THE ROUTE 66 DINING & LODGING GUIDE
15th Edition

Researched by the National Historic Route 66 Federation
Adopt-A-Hundred Program members

Published by the

NATIONAL HISTORIC ROUTE 66 FEDERATION

ISBN 978-0-9709951-7-9

How to get more out of your Route 66 adventure.

As you travel the most legendary byway in America, you will enjoy it more if you take your time. Generations have passed this way and so much of their history remains.

Pick a quiet stretch. Pull over and listen to the pavement sing the bittersweet songs of the Mother Road. Browse through a tiny hamlet that was once a horn-honking, bumper-to-bumper tourist mecca. Savor the soul of an America that is growing harder and harder to find each year.

Like the thousands of travelers who have used this guide before you, it can help you make the most of your adventure by guiding you to the establishments that appeal to you. And, yes, by keeping you out of those that don't. It can also show you how to sample the diverse cultures the road passes through on its way between Chicago and Santa Monica.

The guide is purely a labor of love prepared by our Adopt-A-Hundred members for the single purpose of making your trip enjoyable along their adopted sections. No establishment has paid a cent to be selected.

Please keep in mind however, that the road is an ever-changing mosaic, as are prices, menus, amenities and owners. If you had an unpleasant experience or even a pleasant one, we ask that you let us know.

We at the Federation have dedicated ourselves to the preservation of Route 66 so that you and future generations, can continue to enjoy the adventure.

Have fun,

David Knudson
Executive Director
National Historic Route 66 Federation

Contents:

How to get the most out of your Route 66 adventure....................4

Adopt-A-Hundred Map..6

Adopters...7

How to use this guide...8

Chicago, IL to the outskirts of Pontiac, IL...........................9

Pontiac, IL to the outskirts of Springfield, IL.....................16

Springfield, IL to the outskirts of St. Louis, MO...............24

Springfield, IL to the outskirts of Staunton, IL....................24

St. Louis, MO to the outskirts of Rolla, MO.......................32

Rolla, MO to the outskirts of Springfield, MO....................40

Springfield, MO to the outskirts of Baxter Springs, KS................48

Baxter Springs, KS to the outskirts of Tulsa, OK.......................50

Tulsa, OK to the outskirts of Oklahoma City, OK.................56

Oklahoma City OK to the outskirts of Clinton, OK.................66

Clinton, OK to the outskirts of Shamrock, TX.....................71

Shamrock, TX to the outskirts of Amarillo, TX............................75

Amarillo, TX to the outskirts of Tucumcari, TX...................78

Tucumcari, NM to the outskirts of Santa Rosa, NM...............82

Santa Rosa, NM to the outskirts of Albuquerque, NM................86

Santa Rosa, NM to the outskirts of Santa Fe, NM........................89

Santa Fe, NM to the outskirts of Albuquerque, NM...............92

Albuquerque, NM to the outskirts of Grants, NM...............98

Albuquerque, NM to the outskirts of Mesita, NM.......................105

Grants, NM to the outskirts of Gallup, NM....................................108

Gallup, NM to the outskirts of Winslow, AZ.....................112

Winslow, AZ to the outskirts of Williams, AZ.....................116

Williams, AZ to the outskirts of Hackberry, AZ.....................125

Hackberry, AZ to the outskirts of Needles, CA............................136

Needles, CA to the outskirts of Amboy, CA.......................140

Amboy, CA to the outskirts of Barstow, CA.......................143

Barstow, CA to the outskirts of Claremont, CA...................144

Claremont, CA through Santa Monica, CA...................................154

Our Adopt-A-Hundred Program watches over America's most famous highway.

Each section in the program is approximately 100 miles long and has been adopted by one of our members. Adopters travel their sections periodically and report any preservation problems which may have arisen.

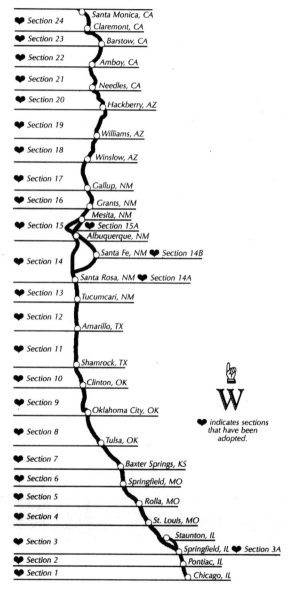

♥ Section 24	Santa Monica, CA
	Claremont, CA
♥ Section 23	Barstow, CA
♥ Section 22	
	Amboy, CA
♥ Section 21	
	Needles, CA
♥ Section 20	
	Hackberry, AZ
♥ Section 19	
	Williams, AZ
♥ Section 18	
	Winslow, AZ
♥ Section 17	
	Gallup, NM
♥ Section 16	Grants, NM
	Mesita, NM
♥ Section 15	♥ Section 15A
	Albuquerque, NM
	Santa Fe, NM ♥ Section 14B
♥ Section 14	
	Santa Rosa, NM ♥ Section 14A
♥ Section 13	Tucumcari, NM
♥ Section 12	
	Amarillo, TX
♥ Section 11	
	Shamrock, TX
♥ Section 10	Clinton, OK
♥ Section 9	
	Oklahoma City, OK
♥ Section 8	
	Tulsa, OK
♥ Section 7	
	Baxter Springs, KS
♥ Section 6	Springfield, MO
♥ Section 5	Rolla, MO
♥ Section 4	
	St. Louis, MO
♥ Section 3	Staunton, IL
	Springfield, IL ♥ Section 3A
♥ Section 2	Pontiac, IL
♥ Section 1	Chicago, IL

W

♥ indicates sections that have been adopted.

Thank you to the following adopters for giving so freely of their time in the preparation of this guide.

- John Weiss
- Dave Clark & Carol Krohn
- Jane Dippel
- Ron Warnick & Emily Priddy
- Mark Potter
- Laura Bennison
- Don Martus
- Phil & Pat Henderson
- James Dawson & Jamie Dawson Kinsey
- Dave Willman
- Beth Coulter
- Tracy Rogers
- Peter Scott
- Barbara Cummins
- Bill Flounders
- Dan Harvey
- Frank Maloney
- Todd Westbrook
- Kevin Curran
- Frank Souers
- Vic Sapphire
- Hal & Nancy Robinson
- Kevin Hansel
- Larry & Jean Mattson

Take along the EZ66 GUIDE For Travelers - the companion to the Route 66 Dining & Lodging Guide.

Get the ultimate guide for finding and exploring the Route. Drive from the WEST or the EAST. Created and richly illustrated by noted Route 66 authority and artist, Jerry McClanahan. Maps and directions are comprehensive yet easy to follow. Also includes attractions, tips, other sources, and games. Spiral bound so it's easy to follow while driving.

$5^{1/2}$" x $8^{1/2}$", 200 page format. Updated regularly.

Published by the National Historic Route 66 Federation.

Order at our website ww.national66.org

How to use this guide.

Historically, travelers have driven east to west on Route 66.

This is simply the tradition because we know the road also goes west to east (although some Californians won't agree). But we won't break with tradition here, so our guide starts in Chicago (Adopt-A-Hundred Section 1) and takes you west to Santa Monica (Adopt-A-Hundred Section 24), detouring down several early Mother Road alignments along the way.

Not every establishment listed is right on old Route 66. Adopters are given the latitude of selecting other facilities if they think an area has very few places to recommend or if a facility is particularly worthwhile.

Price ranges do not include tax.

Lodging Example:

Western Sunrise Motel
11616 N. Cedar Rd. (Route 66)
Litchfield, IL
(800) 332-4136
good, fair, exceptional (overall rating)
$40-$50 *(price range)*
value *(particularly good value)*
dining *(includes a restaurant)*
☆ *(very special, worth making plans to visit)*
Visa, MC *(credit cards accepted)*

Dining Example:

Hazel's Astro Diner
3360 S. Oak St.
Springfield, MO
(417) 323-4040
American *(style of food)*
B, L&D *(serves breakfast, lunch & dinner)*
exceptional, good *(overall rating)*
chicken fried steak *(specialty)*
value *(particularly good value)*
service *(particularly good service)*
atmosphere *(particularly nice atmosphere)*
no smoking *(means the whole facility)*
inexpensive, moderate *(price category)*
☆ *(very special, worth making plans to visit)*
Visa, MC *(credit cards accepted)*

Section 1 - Chicago, IL to the outskirts of Pontiac, IL.

Lodging:

The Congress Plaza Hotel ☆
520 S. Michigan Ave.
Chicago, IL
312-427-3800
www.congressplazahotel.com
good - $109-$189 - nonsmoking rooms - internet connections -
a Chicago original built in 1893 - two blocks from the start/end
of the Route - major cards

Best Western Chicagoland - Countryside
6251 Joliet Rd. (Route 66)
Countryside, IL
708-354-5200
www.hamptoninn.com
exceptional - $90-$95 - includes breakfast bar - pool - some
nonsmoking rooms - the Hampton Inn chain is a strong Route 66
supporter - pets - major cards

La Quinta
855 79th St. (I-55 exit #274)
Willowbrook, IL
630-654-0077
www.laquinta.com
good - $101-$105 - near Dell Rhea's Chicken Basket -
nonsmoking rooms - Continental breakfast - internet
connections - pets - major cards

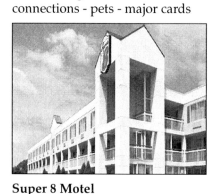

Super 8 Motel
820 W. 79th St.
Willowbrook, IL
630-789-6300
www.super8.com
good - $70 up - near Dell Rhea's Chicken Basket - pool -
Continental breakfast - nonsmoking rooms - internet
connections - pets - major cards

Super 8 Motel
1301 Marquette Dr.
Romeoville, IL
630-759-8880
good - $55- $100 - pets - non smoking rooms - Cont. breakfast -
internet connnections - near the historic White Fence Farm
Restaurant - major cards

Harrah's Casino Hotel
151 N. Joliet St.
Joliet, IL
815-774-2624
good - $59 and up - dining - gaming - non smoking rooms - good
weekday rates - walk to historic Rialto Theatre and the Route 66
Visitor Center - major cards

Braidwood Motel
120 N. Washington St. (at Route 66)
Braidwood, IL
815-458-2321
good - value - $35-$45 - microwaves & fridges - non smoking
rooms - internet connections - laundry next door - cllassic
(restored) motel originally the Rossi Motel - across the tracks
from the famous Polka Dot Drive In - major cards

Super 8 Motel
14 E. Northbrook Dr.
(I-55 exit #220)
Dwight, IL
815-584-1888
www.super8.com
good - value - $40-$45 - major cards

Dining:

☞ *Note - all dining establishments in Illinois are nonsmoking.*

Lou Mitchell's ✰
565 W. Jackson & Jefferson (Route 66 East)
Chicago, IL
312-939-3111
American - exceptional - value - atmosphere - bakery - inexpensive - service - B&L - liquor - Route 66 landmark established in 1923 - major cards

Wolf's Head Inn
6937 Joliet Rd. (Route 66)
Indian Head Park, IL
708-246-0400
American - good - value - atmosphere - L&D Sunday brunch - moderate - walls are filled with fascinating collectibles - liquor - major cards

Dell Rhea's Chicken Basket ☆
645 Joliet Rd. (Route 66)
Willowbrook, IL
630-325-0780
www.chickenbasket.com
American - exceptional - good value - known for fried chicken -
inexpensive - a very special "must stop" - salad bar - L&D - beer -
strong Route 66 supporters - landmark since 1946

White Fence Farm ☆
11700 Joliet Rd. (Route 66 South of I-55)
Romeoville, IL
630-739-1720
www.whitefencefarm.com
American - chicken - exceptional - value - a very special "must
stop" - D Tues. to Sun. closed January - moderate - atmosphere -
ervice - beer - large, free museum and zoo - since the 1920's -
strong Route 66 supporters - major cards

Rich & Creamy ☆
920 N. Broadway St. (Route 66)
Joliet, IL
815- 740 2899
American - ice cream and soft serve creations - a very special
"must stop" - exceptional food, service and atmosphere -
inexpensive - open every day - gateway to the Joliet Route 66
sites - great outdoor displays - overlooks the 1858 Joliet
Correctional Center - only 1 mile from the Route 66 Visitor
Center - no cards

Launching Pad Drive In ☆
Route 53 (Route 66)
Wilmington, IL
815-476-6535
www.launchingpadrt66.com
American - hamburgers - a very special "must stop" - B, L&D -
good - inexpensive - landmark - you can't miss the famous
Gemini Giant in front - strong Route 66 supporters - major cards

Polk-A-Dot Drive-In ☆
Route 53 (Route 66)
Braidwood, IL
815-458-3377www.polk-a-dot.com
American - hamburgers - good - a very special "must stop" -
value - L&D - exceptional 50's & 60's theme - strong Route 66
supporters - major cards

Gardner Restaurant
(Exit 227 from I-55) Route 66
Gardner, IL
815-237-0406
American - home cooking - good - value - B, L & D - moderate -
Visa, MC

Pete's Restaurant & Pancake House
900 N. Union (Route 66 & Route 47)
Dwight, IL
815-584-2331
American - home cooking - good - value - B, L & D -
inexpensive - beer - large portions - Visa, MC

Old Route 66 Family Restaurant
105 S. Old Route 66
Dwight, IL
815-584-2920
American - home cooking - good - value - B, L & D - notice
the mural outside - souvenirs - strong Route 66 supporters -
Visa, MC

Wishing Well Cafe
110 W. Tremont St.
Odell, IL
815-998-2081
American - home cooking - good - B, L & D - inexpensive -
Visa, MC

Pour Richard's
210 Tremont St.
Odell, IL
815-998 2556
American - good - D - nice indoor mural - liquor - inexpensive -
don't miss the famous restored Route 66 filling station in Odell -
strong Route 66 supporters - major cards

Rentz's Tap & Restaurant
210 S. Waupansie St.
Odell, IL
815-998-2383
American - good - inexpensive - L&D - liquor - one block from
the historic Odell gas station - major cards

Section 2 - Pontiac, IL to the outskirts of Springfield, IL.

☞ *When in Pontiac, make sure you visit the exceptional Route 66*
Hall of Fame and Museum.

Lodging:

Super 8
601 S. Deerfield Rd. (IL Rt.116 exit 197 from I-55)
Pontiac, IL
815-844-6888
www.super8.com
good - $55-$69 - Cont. breakfast - pets $15 with permission -
nonsmoking rooms - some fridges & some microwaves - wi-fi
internet connections - Visa, MC, DC, Disc

Holiday Inn Express
1823 W. Reynolds St. (IL Rt.116 exit 197 from I-55)
Pontiac, IL
815-844-4444
www.hiexpress.com
good - $89-$135 - nonsmoking rooms - some fridges, microwaves
and whirlpools - Cont. breakfast - access to fitness club - wi-fi
internet connections - major cards

Three Roses Bed & Breakfast ☆
209 E. Howard St.
Pontiac, IL
815-844-3404
www.3rosesbnb.com
exceptional - $120-$160 - single occupancy - two home cooked
meals a day - discounts for multiple night stays and for Route 66
travelers - advance reservation and deposit normally required - a
very special "must stop" - pets - nonsmoking rooms - internet
connections - just 2 blocks from the IL Route 66 Hall Of Fame &
Museum - great small town feel - Visa, MC

Super 8 Motel
I-55 and US 24 (Exit 187)
Chenoa, IL
815-945-5900
www.super8.com
good - $65-$75 - pets $10 - Cont. breakfast - nonsmoking rooms - wi-fi internet connections - Visa, MC, Disc

Best Western University Inn
6 Trader Circle (I-39 & US 51)
Normal, IL
309-454-4070
www.bestwestern.com
good - from $79 - pool - sauna - pets $10 - Full breakfast - nonsmoking rooms - wi-fi internet connections - major cards

Chateau Hotel & Conference Center
1601 Jumer Dr.
Bloomington, IL
309-662-2020
www.chateauhotel.biz
exceptional - $79-$180 - dining - lounge - pool - pets $25 - some microwaves and fridges - nonsmoking rooms - sauna - fitness center - internet connections - major cards

Super 8 Motel
South & Elm Streets (Exit 145 from I-55)
McLean, IL
309-874-2366 www.super8.com
good - $52-$80 - pool - pets $10 with permission - nonsmoking rooms - Cont. breakfast - fridges & microwaves - some suites with whirlpools - internet connections - across from Dixie Trucker's Home - major cards

Dining:

☞ *Note - all dining establishments in Illinois are nonsmoking.*

Old Log Cabin ☆
18700 Old Route 66
Pontiac, IL
815-842-2908
American - good - memorabilia on display - a very special "must stop" - B, L&D Mon. thru Sat. - liquor - inexpensive - classic 1926 roadhouse - major Route 66 supporters - Visa, MC

Baby Bull's Family Restaurant
Route 116 at I-55 exit 197 (near Route 66 bypass)
Pontiac, IL
815-844-5757
American - good - moderate - B, L&D 7 days - breakfast all day - Visa, MC

La Mex
930 West Custer Ave. (Route 66 bypass and Rt. 23)
Pontiac, IL
815-844-4564
Mexican - fajitas, burritos, chimichangas - exceptional - L&D 7 days - moderate - liquor - major cards

19

Pontiac Family Kitchen
904 Kuster Ave. (near Route 66 bypass and Route 23)
Pontiac, IL
815-844-3155
American - broasted chicken, homemade meatloaf, huge varied
menu - exceptional - value - moderate - B,L&D 7days (open 24
hours on Fri. & Sat.) - liquor - great Route 66 supporters - Bob
Waldmire's artwork on display - major cards

DeLong's Casual Dining
201. N. Mill
Pontiac, IL
815-844-1983
American - sweet potato chips, breaded pork tenderloin
sandwich, chicken pot pie, Angus steak burgers, frozen custard,
Prime rib on Fri. & Sat. eves - good - inexpensive - L&D - Mon.
thru Sat., beer & wine - Visa, MC

Bernardi's
1234 N. Mill
(2 blocks suth of the Route 66 Museum)
Pontiac, IL
815-842-1198
www.BernardiRestaurants.com
Italian & American - fried chicken, tortellini, spaghetti -
exceptional - value - service - moderate - L&D - Tues. thru Sun. -
liquor - major cards

Filling Station Cafe
Route 66 & Main St.
Lexington, IL
309-365-8813
American - good - B, L&D 7 days - moderate - Visa, MC

Avanti's Italian Restaurant
407 S. Main
Normal, IL
309-452-4436 www.avantisnormal.com
Italian - pizza, pasta, sandwiches, salad, their signature dish is
the Gondola Sandwich - good - moderate - L&D - 7 days -
liquor - Visa, MC

Keller's Iron Skillet
609 Hannah St. (US 150 south of Oakland Ave.)
Bloomington, IL
309-828-3533 www.kellersironskillet.com
American - breakfast combos, steaks & chops, Friday night
catfish special - good - moderate - B 7 days, L Mon. thru Sat.,
D Fri. only - located in the former Steak 'n' Shake building
southeast of downtown Bloomington - Visa, MC

Lucca Grill ☆
116 E. Market St. (NW corner of Market & NB BUS 51 (Route 66)
Bloomington, IL
309-828-7521 www.luccagrill.com
Italian/American - pizza, pasta, sandwiches - exceptional -
moderate - a very special "must stop" - open since 1936, the first
pizzeria in the midwest - in a historic building in downtown
Bloomington - L & D 7 days - liquor - major cards

Biaggi's Ristorante Italiano
1501 N. Veteran's Parkway
Bloomington, IL
309-661-8322
www.biaggis.com
Italian - pasta, soups, fried ravioli, chicken, veal, beef, seafood -
expensive - exceptional - L&D 7days - liquor - major cards

Country-Aire Restaurant
606 W. South St. (west of I-55 exit 140 on Rt. 25)
Atlanta, IL
217-648-5330
American - good - moderate - B, L & D 7 days - Visa, MC, Disc

Palm Grill Cafe ☆
110 Arch St.
Atlanta, IL
217-648-2233
American - breakfast served all day - sandwiches, daily blue
plate specials, pie, sundaes - a very special "must stop" - good -
inexpensive - atmosphere - B,L&D 7 days - historic 1930s
Route 66 diner that was restored and re-opened in 2009 - Visa,
MC, Disc

Guzzardo's Italian Villa
509 Pulaski (at Kickapoo St.)
Lincoln, IL
217-732-6370
Italian/American - large portions, excellent soup & salad bar,
steaks & prime rib - good - L&D Tues. thru Sat. - moderate -
major cards

Hallie's On The Square
111 S. Kickapoo St. (at Broadway St.)
Lincoln, IL
217-732-6923
German/American - "home of the Schnitzel since 1945" - good -
moderate - L&D Mon. thru Sat. - no cards

Section 3 - Springfield, IL to the outskirts of St. Louis, MO & Section 3A - Springfield, IL to Staunton, IL.

Lodging:

Super 8
1330 S. Dirksen Parkway
Springfield, IL
217-528-8889
www.super8.com
good - $55 - pets - some fridges & microwaves - nonsmoking
rooms - Cont. breakfast - laundry - wi-fi internet connections -
major cards

Route 66 Hotel & Conference Center ☆☆
625 E. St. Joseph St. (S. 6th St. & Stevenson Dr.)
Springfield, IL
Toll free (888) 707-8366
www.rt66hotel.com
good - a very special "must stop" - $66-$150 - dining - pool - pets
$50 deposit - internet connections - some microwaves & fridges -
nonsmoking rooms - passes to nearby fitness center - exceptional
Rt. 66 and vintage vehicle theme decor - gift shop - strong Route
66 supporters - major cards

Mansion View Inn & Suites
529 S. Fourth St.
Springfield, IL
217-544-7411
www.mansionview.com
good - $89-$139 - pets $25 - nonsmoking rooms - Cont.
breakfast - internet connections - access to fitness club -
microwaves & fridges in suites - convenient to downtown
attractions - major cards

Carlin Villa Motel
18891 Route 4 (1926-1930 Route 66 alignment)
Carlinville, IL
217-854-3201 www.carlinvillaon66.com
good - value - $44-$122 - Cont. breakfast - nonsmoking rooms -
game room - seasonal pool - pets $6 - meeting rooms - some
microwaves & fridges - whirlpool - tanning beds - internet
connections - fax & copier available - major cards

Best Western Carlinville Inn
I-55 & Route 108 (Exit 60) Post 1930 Route 66 alignment
Carlinville, IL
217324-2100 www.bestwestern.com
exceptional - $89-$109 - dining - free full breakfast - year round
pool - pets $15 - all nonsmoking rooms - wi-fi internet
connections in rooms - microwaves and fridges in some rooms -
nicely landscaped - stationary paddlewheel boat can be rented -
Route 66 souvenirs - major cards

Art's Motel
101 Main St. (I-55 exit 72 at Rt 17)
Farmersville, IL
217-227-3277
good - $45 incl. tax - pets $5 - nonsmoking rooms - note the
vintage sign restored with the help of the IL Route 66
Assoc. - internet connections in rooms - Visa, MC, Disc -
no checks

Comfort Inn
3080 South State (Rt 157, Route 66))
Edwardsville, IL
www.comfortinn.com
618-656-4900
exceptional - $80-$95 - pool - nonsmoking rooms - Cont.
breakfast - fitness room - coffee and microwave in lobby - wi-fi
internet connections - strong Route 66 supporters - major cards

Dining:

☞ *Note - all dining establishments in Illinois are nonsmoking.*

Coney Island
210 S. 5th St.
Springfield, IL
217-522-2050
American - chili dogs & pony shoes - exceptional - inexpensive -
L &D Mon. thru Sat. - walk up window open for carry-out Fri. &
Sat. eves - exceptional neon sign - founded 1919 - no cards

Cozy Drive In ☆
2936 S. 6th (Route 66)
Springfield, IL
217-525-1992
www.cozydogdrivein.com
American - the restaurant that perfected the corn dog - B, L&D
Mon. thru Sat. - exceptional - value - service - inexpensive -
a special "must stop" - strong Route 66 supporters -
atmosphere - souvenirs - wonderful collection of Route 66
memorabilia - lots of artwork by the founder's son, Bob
Waldmire - no cards

Yesterday's Restaurant
625 E. St Joseph St. (S. 6th St. & Stevenson Dr.)
Springfield, IL
888-707-8366
www.rt66hotel.com
American - good - value - moderate - BL&D Mon. thru Sat. -
liquor - Route 66 theme diner in the Route 66 Hotel &
Conference Center - major cards

La Fiesta
2830 Stevenson Dr.
Springfield, IL
217-585-6767
Mexican - fajitas, burritos, combination plates - exceptional -
moderate - L & D 7 days, lunch specials Mon. thru Sat. - liquor -
major cards

Charlie Parker's Diner
700 North St.
Springfield, IL
217-241-2104
www.charlieparkersdiner.net
American - breakfast, classic diner fare, horseshoes -
exceptional - value - moderate - B&L 7 days - featured on
"Diners, Drive-Ins & Dives" - major cards

Whirla-Whip ☆
309 S. 3rd St.
(Illinois 4, 1 block south of 1926-1930 Route 66 alignment)
Girard, IL
217-627-3210
www.whirlawhip.com
American - 1000 flavors of soft serve ice cream, burgers,
horseshoes - good - a special "must stop" - L&D, 7 days - open
April thru September at this location since 1957 - no cards

Reno's Pizza and Ristorante
518 North Side Square
(1926-1930 Route 66 alignment
Carlinville, IL
217-854-6655
Italian - pizza and pasta, homemade lasagna - exceptional - value - moderate - L&D Tues. thru Sun. - liquor - beautiful trompe l'oeil murals on the walls and ceiling - Visa, MC

Ariston Cafe ☆
Old Route 66 & Route 16
Litchfield, IL
217-324-2023
www.ariston-cafe.com
American/Greek/Continental - steaks, burgers, fried chicken, Sunday Buffet - exceptional - a very special "must stop" - moderate - L&D 7 days - atmosphere - service - salad bar - liquor - strong Route 66 supporters - landmark established 1924, run by the same family - historic neon sign - major cards

Stacey's
318 S. Historic Route 66
Litchfield, IL
217-324-2771
American - breakfast, burgers, horseshoes - homestyle cooking -
good - inexpensive - beer & wine - B, L&D 7 days - salad bar -
no cards

Crossroads
I-55 and Route 138 (I-55 exit 44)
Mt. Olive, IL
217-999-3688
American - dinner specials - chicken gizzards, ham & beans,
homemade pies - good - inexpensive - B, L&D 7 days - no cards

Decamp Junction
8767 State Route 4
Staunton, IL
618-637-2951
American - pizza - good - inexpensive - D Wed. thru Sun. -
liquor - lots of memorabilia in historic Route 66 roadhouse -
strong Route 66 supporters - liquor - Visa, MC

Bella Milano
1063 S. State Route 157
(Route 66)
Edwardsville, IL
618-659-2100
Italian - veal, pizza & calzones - exceptional -
moderate - atmosphere - service - L&D 7 days - early
dining specials Mon. thru Thurs. 4:30-6 pm - liquor -
major cards

Itty-Bitty Restaurant
512 E. Chain of Rocks Rd.
(Route 66)
Mitchell, IL
618-797-1337
American/Mexican/Italian - strawberry
shortcake - homestyle cooking, "no heat lamps
or microwaves" - good - value - inexpensive -
B Mon. thru Fri., L&D Mon. thru Sat. - no cards

Luna Cafe ☆
201 E. Chain of Rocks Rd.
(Route 66)
Mitchell, IL
618-931-3152
American - good - inexpensive - a special "must stop" - L&D 7
days - free chicken wings on Mon. and Thurs. - liquor - classic
Route 66 roadhouse - great neon sign - one of the oldest
businesses on 66 - no cards

Section 4 - St. Louis, MO to the outskirts of Rolla, MO.

Lodging:

Hampton Inn At The Arch
333 Washington Ave. (On a 1950's alignment of Route 66)
St. Louis, MO
314-621-7900
www.hamptoninn.com
exceptional - $98-$149 - pool - nonsmoking rooms - Full
breakfast - gift shop - fitness room - internet connections in
rooms - dining - laundry - beautiful lobby with vintage photos of
old St. Louis - great views from rooms of the Mississippi River,
St. Louis skyline and the Gateway Arch - major cards

Best Western Kirkwood Inn
1200 S. Kirkwood Rd.
(Bypass 66)
St. Louis, MO
314-821-3950
www.bestwestern.com/kirkwoodinn
exceptional - $110-$120 - deluxe breakfast buffet free to guests -
internet connections - pool - pets - completely remodeled in
2006 - nonsmoking rooms - major cards

Wayside Motel
7800 Watson Rd.
(Route 66)
Webster Groves, MO
314-961-2324
fair - $50-$55 - nonsmoking rooms - vintage motel near the site of
the razed Coral Court - Visa, MC, Disc

Travelodge Diamond Inn Motel
2875 Hwy. 100
(Route 66) at I-44 exit 253
Villa Ridge, MO
636-742-3501
good - $69-79 - pool - pets - Cont. Breakfast - nonsmoking
rooms - internet connections - major cards

Budget Lodging
866 S. Outer Rd.
St. Clair, MO
636-629-1000 800-958-4354 www.budgetlodging.com
exceptional - $59-$79 - value - deluxe Cont. breakfast - pets $10 -
seasonal pool - coffee, tea & popcorn in lobby - some fridges &
microwaves - wi-fi internet connections in rooms - nonsmoking
rooms - Jacuzzi and 5 bdrm. cabin available - Visa, MC, Disc

Stanton Motel
I-44 exit 230 (North Outer Rd.)
Stanton, MO
573-590-4247
fair - $35-$53 - nonsmoking rooms - vintage motel - nonsmoking
rooms - Visa, MC

Comfort Inn
736 S. Service Rd. West
Sullivan, MO
573-468-7800 www.choicehotels.com
exceptional - $89 up - Deluxe Cont. Breakfast - pool - fridges,
microwaves, hair dryers, coffee makers, irons & boards -
nonsmoking rooms - fitness & meeting rooms - laundry -
internet connections - major cards

Family Motor Inn
209 N. Service Rd. (Hwy. 185 between I-44 exits 225 and 226)
Sullivan, MO
573-468-4119
fair - $45-$55 - pool - pets - Cont. Breakfast - nonsmoking rooms -
Visa, MC, Disc

Budget Inn Motel
55 Hwy. C (at I-44 exit 218)
Bourbon, MO
573-732-4080
www.budgetinn.com
fair - $37-$45 - large rooms - nonsmoking rooms - pets -
Visa, MC, Disc

Best Western Cuba Inn
246 Hwy. P (N. of I-44 exit 208, East of Hwy. 19)
Cuba, MO
573-885-7707
www.bestwestern.com
exceptional - value - $66-$125 - pool - pets $10 - nonsmoking
rooms - deluxe full, hot breakfast buffet - internet connections -
Visa, MC, Disc

Wagon Wheel Motel ☆
901 E. Washington St.
Cuba, MO
573-885-3411
www.wagonwheel66cuba.com
exceptional - a special "must stop" - $66-$110 - pets -
nonsmoking rooms - wi-fi internet connection in rooms - flat
screen tvs - pillow top beds - gift shop - beautifully restored and
renovated historic Route 66 motel - Visa, MC

Dining:

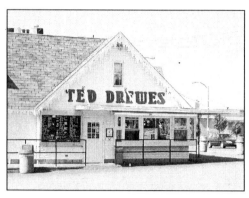

Ted Drewes Frozen Custard
6726 Chippewa (Route 66)
St. Louis, MO
314-482-2652
www.teddrewes.com
American - frozen custard, cones, malts, sundaes, shakes - famous for shakes known as "concrete", so thick they can be turned upside down without falling out of the cup - exceptional -value - inexpensive - L&D 7 days - smoking - a Route 66 landmark since 1929 - no inside seating - Visa, MC

Eat-Rite Diner
622 Chouteau Ave.
St. Louis, MO
314-621-9621
American diner fare - cheeseburgers - good - value - inexpensive - BL&D 7 days - smoking - no cards

Tigin Irish Pub
333 Washington Ave.
(a 1950s alignment of Route 66)
St. Louis, MO
314-241-8666
www.tiginirishpub.com
Irish - boxty (Irish potato cakes or crepes), shepherd's pie,
bangers & mash (mashed potatoes & Irish sausage) -
exceptional - moderate - L&D 7 days - smoking - liquor - in the
same building as the Hampton Inn at the Arch, space was
originally occupied by Trader Vic's in the 1950s - major cards

Trainwreck Saloon
9243 Manchester Rd. (original Route 66)
Rock Hill, MO
314-962-8148
www.trainwrecksaloon.com
American - sandwiches, burgers, salads - good - moderate -
atmosphere - L&D 7 days - liquor - located in the oldest
continually operated tavern in St. Louis County - train theme -
features a beer garden built around a caboose - smoking - major cards

Hacienda Mexican Restaurant

9748 Manchester Rd. (original Route 66)
Rock Hill, MO
314-962-7100 www.hacienda-stl.com
Mexican - margaritas, fajitas, salads - good - moderate -
atmosphere - L&D 7 days - smoking - liquor - in historic 1861
building - beautiful outdoor patio with fountain - major cards

Spencer's Grill

223 S. Kirkwood Rd. (bypass Route 66)
Kirkwood, MO
314-821-2601
American diner fare - good - inexpensive - BL&D Tues. thru
Sat. - great neon sign, classic 1947 diner - smoking - Visa, MC

Lewis Cafe

145 S. Main St. (1 mile south of I-44 exit 240)
St. Clair, MO
636-629-9975
American - farm raised Angus beef steaks and burgers, home
made pies, salad with their own "famous home made poppy
seed dressing" - do all their own baking - exceptional -
inexpensive - value - old style downtown cafe since 1938 -
atmosphere - B, L&D 7 days - smoking - Visa, MC, Disc

Los Cabos
1909 N. Service Rd.
(north of I-44 exit 240, east of Rt. 47)
St. Clair, MO
636-629-0068
Mexican - Cabos fried tacos, chicken, staek, seafood, fajitas -
good - L&D 7 days - moderate - liquor - smoking - Visa, MC, Disc

Circle Inn Malt Shop
171 S. Old Route 66
Bourbon, MO
573-732-4470
American diner fare - pizza, burgers, cakes, soft serve ice cream -
good - value - inexpensive - smoking - B, L&D Mon. thru Sat. -
no credit cards

Missouri Hick Bar-B-Q
913 E. Washington
(Route 66)
Cuba, MO
573-885-6791
American - smoked meats - exceptional - L&D 7 days -
moderate - beer & wine - smoking - Visa, MC, Disc

Route 66 Cafe
510 W. Washington
(Route 66)
Cuba, MO
573-885-1522
American - home style cooking - whole fried catfish - in house baking - good - B&L Mon. thru Sat. - inexpensive - smoking - no cards

Johnnie's Bar
225 N. Jefferson
(Route 66)
St. James, MO
573-265-8223
American - half pound burgers, homemade daily specials - good - value - inexpensive - L&D Mon. thru Sat. - liquor - friendly Route 66 tavern - no credit cards

Section 5 - Rolla, MO to the outskirts of Springfield, MO.

Lodging:

Zeno's Motel & Steakhouse
1621 Martin Springs Dr. (Route 66)
Rolla, MO
573-364-1301 www.zenos.biz
good - $52.47-$63.63 (mention Route 66 for these rates) - dining -
outdoor pool - nonsmoking rooms - 3rd generation family
owned in its 50th year - major cards

Best Western Coachlight
1403 Martin Springs Dr. (Route 66)
Rolla, MO
573-341-2511
www.bestwestern.com
good - $74-$79 - pool - some rooms with small fridges -
small pets - free movies - major cards

Hampton Inn
103 St. Robert Plaza
St. Robert, MO
573-336-3355 www.ehrhardtproperties.com
exceptional - $114-$174 - pool - microwaves - fridges -
nonsmoking rooms - Cont. breakfast - exceptional decor
and staff - Circle of Excellence Award - the chain is a strong
Route 66 supporter - major cards

Montis Best Western
14086 Hwy Z (Route 66)
St. Robert, MO
573-336-4299
good - $65-$75 - restaurant next door - pool - nonsmoking
rooms - Cont. Breakfast - nice, small Best Western - major cards

Munger Moss Motel ☆

1336 Route 66
Lebanon, MO
417-532-3111
www.mungermoss.com
exceptional - value - $37-$52 - a Mother Road icon - a special
"must stop" - pool -nonsmoking rooms - Rt. 66 theme rooms -
over 3 decades of the same management - beautiful grounds -
strong 66 supporters - souvenir shop - major cards

Best Western Wyota Inn

1225 Millcreek Rd. (I44 exit 130)
Lebanon, MO
417-532-6171
www.bestwestern.com
good - $65-$90 - small pets - dining - pool - full breakfast - some
microwaves & fridges - hair dryers, coffee pots, irons & boards
upon request - nice grounds - major cards

Historic Route 66 Inn

1710 W. Elm
Lebanon, MO
417-532-3128
good - $39-$49 - remodeled 2006 - next door to Gary's Catfish &
BBQ - some pets - HBO - nonsmoking rooms - major cards

Dining:

Maid Rite

1028 Kingshighway (Route 66)
Rolla, MO www.maid-rite.com
fast food - good - value - inexpensive - L&D - nonsmoking
section - owned by same family for 32 years - no cards

Zeno's Motel & Steakhouse

1621 Martin Springs Dr. (Route 66)
Rolla, MO
573-364-1301 www.zenos.biz
American - steaks - exceptional - moderate - atmosphere -
service - B, L&D - smoking in lounge only - liquor - 3rd
generation family owned since 1957 - major cards

Great Wall Restaurant
1505 Bishop St. (Route 66)
Rolla, MO
573-341-9922
Chinese - good - inexpensive - traditional peaceful atmosphere -
L&D - beer & wine - nonsmoking section - free delivery - Visa,
MC, Disc

Hickory Pit BBQ
201 W. Hwy. 72
Rolla, MO
573-364-4838
American BBQ ribs, burnt ends, ham, pork, sausage, beef -
good - salad bar - liquor - carryout - L&D - moderate -
nonsmoking section - Visa & MC

Sirloin Stockade
1401 Martin Springs Dr. (Route 66)
Rolla, MO
573-364-7168
American - good - moderate - L&D 7 days - salad bar - smoking -
look for the big bull on the roof - Visa, MC, Disc

Tommy's Tater Patch ☆
103 Bridge School Rd.
Rolla, MO
573-368-3111
American/Tex Mex - pork tenderloin & specialty taters - good -
value - inexpensive - a special "must stop"- atmospher - service -
BL&D 7 days - smoking - liquor - major cards

Cookin' From Scratch
90 Truman (I-44 exit179)
Doolittle, MO
573-762-3111
American - good - value - inexpensive - nonsmoking section -
travel needs store - major cards

Elbow Inn Bar & BBQ Pit
Devil's Elbow, MO
573-336-5375
American BBQ - good - L&D - inexpensive - atmosphere - said to
be the oldest continuous restaurant on Missouri 66 - liquor -
major cards

Sweetwater BBQ
14076 Hwy. 2 (Route 66)
St. Robert, MO
573-336-8830
American hickory smoked bbq ribs, pulled pork, beef, sausage, turkey, ham, chicken - good - moderate - atmosphere - L&D - major cards

Country Cafe
Jct. Hwys 28 & 44 - Hwy. ZZ
(Route 66)
St. Robert, MO
314-366-5200
American - home cooked - good - B,L&D - next door to Montis Best Western - one of the good old Route 66 cafes that keeps on going - Visa & MC

Bell Restaurant
1180 Millcreek Rd.
(Route 66)
Lebanon, MO
417-588-2587
American home cooking - inexpensive - nice Route 66 decor - 50 years on the Mother Road - B, L&D - nonsmoking section - no cards

Faye's Diner
691 W. Elm
(Route 66)
Lebanon, MO
417-532-7338
American home cooking - good - nice diner atmosphere -
inexpensive - B&L - M-F 6 am thru 2 pm - Visa, MC, Disc

Gary's Catfish & BBQ
1760 W. Elm
(Route 66)
Lebanon, MO
417-532-1777
American - steaks, seafood, bbq, catfish - good - moderate -
L&D - atmosphere - no smoking - major cards

Starlite Lanes
1331 E. Route 66
Lebanon, MO
417-532-4262
American - pizza, burgers, tacos, salads - good - inexpensive -
atmosphere - across the street from the Munger Moss Motel -
L&D 7 days - smoking - beer & wine - major cards

Britt's Route 66 Grill ☆
135 Wrinkle Ave. (Route 66)
Lebanon, MO
417-588-3000
American - BBQ, seafood, steaks - smoked meats,
mouthwatering prime rib - salad bar - good - a special "must
stop" - inexpensive to moderate opened as Wrink's Market June
10, 1950 - BBQs outside on Saturdays - L&D - Mon. thru Sat.
10:30 AM to 8 PM; Fri. & Sat. 10:30 AM to 9 PM; closed Sundays -
no smoking - major cards

J's Family Dining
I-44 exit 127
Lebanon, MO
417-588-2281
American - home cooked - good - moderate - B,L&D 7 days -
nonsmoking section - a classic old truck stop - nice 50s decor -
Visa & MC

Rocking Chair Restaurant
105 Martingale Dr. (exit 113)
Conway, MO
417-589-6191
American - home cooking - plate lunches - comfortable - good -
moderate - L&D 7 days - nonsmoking section - Visa & MC

C & C Kuntry
101 E. Pine St.
Strafford, MO
417-736-9222
American - home cooking - homemade cakes & pies - good -
inexpensive - BL&D 7 days - short block off 66 - no smoking -
Visa, MC & Disc

Joe's Diner
201 E. Chestnut
Strafford, MO
417-736-2922
American - tasty burgers & homemade onion rings - good -
inexpensive - L&D Mon. thru Fri. 10:30 am thru 7 pm - closed
Sun. - no smoking - no cards

Section 6 - Springfield, MO to the outskirts of Baxter Springs, KS.

Lodging:

Best Western Coach House Inn
2535 N. Glenstone Ave. (Route 66)
Springfield, MO
417-862-0701
www.bestwestern.com
good - $69-$129 - value - dining - deluxe Cont. breakfast -
playground - some fridges and microwaves - some Jacuzzi
suites - free laundry - 2 pools - DVD players - some nonsmoking
rooms - free wireless internet connections - major cards

Best Western Route 66 Rail Haven
203 S. Glenstone Ave.
(Route 66)
Springfield, MO
417-866-1963 www.route66railhaven.com
good - $60-$126 - Cont. breakfast - many restaurants nearby -
pool & spa - some nonsmoking rooms - some microwaves &
fridges - Mother Road icon - some Jacuzzi suites with hot tubs -
some 50's theme rooms - some internet connections - listed on
the Natl. Register of Historic Places - major cards

Rest Haven Court
2000 E. Kearny (Route 66)
Springfield, MO
417-869-9114
fair - $30-$50 - Cont. breakfast - restaurant next door - pool -
small dogs - internet connections - some nonsmoking rooms -
some microwaves & fridges - sign dates back to1947 -
major cards

La Quinta
3320 Range Line Rd. (Route 66)
Joplin, MO
417-781-0500
www.laquinta.com
good - $79-$90 - small pets - full breakfast - 1 indoor & 1 outdoor
pool - nonsmoking rooms - wireless internet - some whirlpool
tubs - laundry - microwaves & fridges - business center with 2
computers for guests - major cards

Dining:

George's Steak Restaurant
339 S. Glenstone (Route 66)
Springfield, MO
417-831-6777
Mexican/American - great burrito omlet and salsa - good -
value - B, L&D - salad bar - nonsmoking section - inexpensive -
major cards

Bamboo Gardens
202 N. Garrison
Carthage, MO
417-358-1611
Chinese - good - L&D - salad bar and large buffet - moderate - nice
change from road fare - no smoking - no checks - major cards

Bradbury Bishop Deli
201 N. Main (Route 66)
Webb City, MO
417-673-4047
American - good - B&L - inexpensive - Closed Sunday - old
fashioned soda fountain - building opened in 1887 - no
smoking - Visa, MC

Jim Bob's Steak and Ribs
2040 S. Range Line Rd. (Route 66)
Joplin, MO
417-781-3300
American - steak and BBQ - exceptional - atmosphere - L&D -
moderate - beer & wine - nonsmoking section - major cards

Granny Shaffer's
2728 N. Range Line Rd. (Route 66)
Joplin, MO
417-659-9393
American - fried chicken and catfish, great gooseberry pie -
good - value - B, L&D - inexpensive - nonsmoking section -
major cards

Eisler Bros. General Store
Route 66
Riverton, KS
316-848-3330www.eislerbros.com
sandwiches - full deli - good - inexpensive - landmark - extensive
gift and souvenir shop - soda fountain - since 1925 - major cards

Section 7 - Baxter Springs, KS to the outskirts of Tulsa, OK.
Lodging:

Little Brick Inn
1101 Military Ave. (Route 66)
Baxter Springs, KS
620-856-5646 www.thelittlebrickinn.com
good - $65-$85 – pets – microwaves & fridges in guest area – full
breakfast – nonsmoking rooms – wireless Internet in rooms –
laundry available – dining downstairs in the "Café on the Route"
restaurant – special events can be accommodated at Café on the
Route – major cards

Baxter Inn-4-Less
2451 Military Ave. (Route 66)
Baxter Springs, KS
620-856-2106 or 866-856-9820
good – $40-$80 – pets – microwaves & fridges – nonsmoking
rooms – free wi-fi – flat-screen TVs – free local calls – Continental
breakfast – coffee – suites available – many discounts – truck
parking – restaurant next door – major cards

Miami Super 8 Motel
2120 Steve Owens Blvd.
Miami, OK
918-542-3382 www.super8.com
good – value - $51.99-$59.99 – pool – pets with $10 fee –
microwaves & fridges – nonsmoking rooms – Continental
breakfast – wi-fi Internet connection in rooms – handicap
accessible rooms available – fax – hot tub – safes in rooms –
in-room coffee – major cards

Inn of Miami
2225 E. Steve Owens Blvd.
Miami, OK
918-542-6681
good - $59.50-$64.50 – pool – pets – microwaves & fridges –
nonsmoking rooms – Internet connection in rooms –
full-service restaurant – in-room coffee – irons and ironing
boards – major cards

Route 66 Motel of Afton
US 59 & 69 (1 1/4 mi. east of Afton)
Afton, OK
918-257-8313
good – $40-$45 – pets with $10 fee – microwaves & fridges –
nonsmoking rooms – Internet – theme rooms – across from
Buffalo Ranch – major cards

Relax Inn
110 W. Dwain Willis Ave.
(Route 66)
Vinita, OK
918-256-6492
good – value - $40-$70 – pets – microwaves & fridges –
nonsmoking rooms – wireless Internet – in-room coffee – fax –
three-bedrooms available – shampoo, snacks and other items
sold in office – major cards

Western Motel
437866 E. Hwy. 66
Vinita, OK
918-256-7542
fair – value - $34.50-$45 – pets – microwaves & fridges –
nonsmoking rooms – next door to Hi-Way Café – major cards

Park Hills Motel & RV Park
1 mile west of Vinita on Route 66
Vinita, OK
918-256-5511
good – value - $20 for RVs; $35-$45 for rooms – pets –
microwaves & fridges – laundry – wi-fi Internet – in-room
coffee – horseshoes – volleyball – pond – RV park – full hookup –
30/50 amp service – meeting/game room available – Visa, MC

Chelsea Motor Inn
325 E. Layton St. (Route 66)
Chelsea, OK
918-789-3437
good – $43.60-$49.05 – microwaves & fridges – nonsmoking
rooms – Internet connection – Visa, MC, Discover – strong Route
66 supporters – meet their three pet donkeys – teepee available
during warm-weather months – Visa, MC, Discover

Claremore Motor Inn
1709 N. Lynn Riggs Blvd. (Route 66)
Claremore, OK
918-342-4545 or 800-828-4540
www.cmi66.com
exceptional – value - $44-$70 – pets – microwaves & fridges in all
rooms – nonsmoking rooms – Continental breakfast – Internet
connection in rooms – computer in lobby – laundry on
premises – dry cleaning available – many discounts – irons &
ironing boards – hair dryers – fax – copier – suites – free
newspapers – drinks and snacks available – safes in rooms –
coffee machines – strong Route 66 supporters – major cards

Will Rogers Inn
940 S. Lynn Riggs (Route 66)
Claremore, OK
918-341-4410
www.magnusonhotels.com/will-rogers-inn-claremore
good - $62-$67 – pool – pets – some full kitchens – microwaves &
fridges – nonsmoking rooms – Continental breakfast – some
suites available – Internet in rooms – laundry on premises –
restaurant and bar attached – major cards

Dining:

Café on the Route
1101 Military Ave. (Route 66)
Baxter Springs, KS
620-856-5646 www.cafeontheroute.com
American – fried potato salad, catfish, brisket, twice-baked
potatoes – exceptional – a must-stop – moderate – atmosphere –
service – L&D Mon.-Sat.; B&L only on Sun. –beer/wine – in the
Little Brick Inn. Originally the Crowell Ban, which was held up
by Jesse James in 1876 – friendly owner and staff – featured on
"Diners, Drive-Ins and Dives"– major cards

Baxter Springs Smokehouse
2320 S. Military Ave. (Route 66)
Baxter Springs, KS
620-856-EATS
www.baxterspringsbbq.com
Barbecue – good – inexpensive – L&D Mon.-Fri.; 7 a.m.-9 p.m.
Sat.; 8 a.m.-2 p.m. Sun. – Visa, MC, Discover

Waylan's Ku-Ku
915 Main (Route 66)
Miami, OK
918-542-1696
American – burgers – good – inexpensive – L&D 7 days – no
smoking – Route 66 décor – cruise nights on fourth Saturday
April thru Sept. – ask for a free map to the "Spook Light" –
strong Route 66 supporters – major cards

Pizza Hut Express
101A NW
(behind Coleman Theatre)
Miami, OK
918-540-2471
pizza – good – inexpensive – fun 1950s Route 66 décor – L&D –
7 days – no smoking – Visa, MC

Clanton's Café
319 E. Illinois (Route 66)
Vinita, OK
918-256-9053
www.clantonscafe.com
American – great breakfasts – chicken-fried steak – good –
inexpensive – B, L&D Mon. thru Fri.; B&L Sat.; L only Sun. – no
smoking – same family has owned Clanton's since the Mother
Road was born – major cards

Chuck Wagon Restaurant
27501 S. 4380 Rd.
Vinita, OK
918-256-3180
www.cowboyjunction.org
American – steaks – good – moderate – atmosphere –
L&D Mon. thru Sat. (close at 7 p.m. Mon.) – salad bar –
no smoking – cowboy-themed restaurant is owned by attached
church – Visa, MC, Disc

Prairie Rose Grille
1102 Walnut
Chelsea, OK
918-789-5111
American – burgers, diner food – good – cute atmosphere –
inexpensive – B, L&D 7 days – no smoking – major cards

Top Hat Dairy Bar
Route 66 & 28A
(east end of town)
Foyil, OK
918-341-0477
American – burgers – good – inexpensive – B, L&D – 7 days –
no smoking – Visa, MC

Cotton-Eyed Joe's
715 Moretz
Claremore, OK
918-342-0855
American – barbecue – good – moderate – L&D Mon.-Sat. –
no smoking – beer – major cards

Molly's Landing
Route 66 between Claremore and Catoosa
Catoosa, OK
918-266-7853 www.mollyslanding.com
American – exceptional - upscale dining – expensive –
atmosphere – service – D – closed Sundays – no smoking –
liquor – major cards

Section 8 - From Tulsa, OK to the outskirts of Oklahoma City, OK.

Lodging:

Desert Hills Motel
5220 E. 11th St. (Route 66)
Tulsa, OK
918-834-3311www.deserthillstulsa.com
fair - $40-$52 – nonsmoking rooms – wi-fi – laundry –
beautifully restored neon sign – unique architecture –
major cards

The Ambassador Hotel
1324 S. Main St.
Tulsa, OK
888-408-8282 or 918-587-8200
www.hotelambassador-tulsa.com
exceptional - $179-$269 – Chalkboard restaurant attached –
pets – fridges – nonsmoking rooms – Internet – laundry –
fitness center – safes – in-room coffee – irons and ironing
boards – hairdryers – helpful staff – built in 1929 as
extended-stay lodging for millionaires and oil barons; on
National Register of Historic Places – optional shuttle
service – major cards

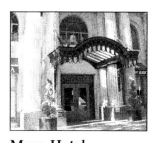

Mayo Hotel
105 W. Fifth St.
Tulsa, OK
918-582-6296
www.themayohotel.com
exceptional - $159-$235 – full kitchens available –
microwaves & fridges – nonsmoking rooms – Internet –
dry-cleaning service available – robes – in-room safes –
built 1925; renovated 2009 – on National Register of
Historic Places – on-site museum – restaurant, coffeehouse,
and penthouse bar on premises – major cards

Cedar Rock Inn
4501 W. 41st St.
Tulsa, OK
918-447-4493 or 877-446-4493
www.cedarrockinn.com
exceptional - $195-$295 – fridge – nonsmoking rooms –
full breakfast – Internet – walking trail – library –
complimentary soft drinks and water – fireplaces – gift
shop – event center on premises – part of the Perryman
home/complex dating to 1890 – major cards

Skyliner Motel
717 W. Main (Route 66)
Stroud, OK
918-968-9556
good - $48-$65 – microwaves & fridges – nonsmoking rooms – Internet – coffee – historic neon sign out front – major cards

Lincoln Motel
740 E. First St. (Route 66)
Chandler, OK
405-258-0200
good - $35-$65 – microwaves & fridges – nonsmoking rooms – Internet – currently undergoing restoration – historic neon sign out front – major cards

Dining:

58

Hank's Hamburgers ☆
8933 E. Admiral Place (1926 alignment of Route 66)
Tulsa, OK
918-832-1509 www.hankshamburgers.com
American – hamburgers, peanut butter balls –
exceptional – value – a special "must-stop" – inexpensive –
L Mon.; L&D Tues. thru Sat. – no smoking – try the Big
Okie: four quarter-pound beef patties layered with cheese
and the works – Visa, MC, Disc

Ike's Chili House
5941 E. Admiral Place (1926 alignment of Route 66)
Tulsa, OK
918-838-9410
chili – exceptional – inexpensive – L&D Mon. thru Fri., L
only on Sat. – no smoking – since 1908 – Visa, MC, Disc

Blue Dome Diner
313 E. Second St. (1926 alignment of Route 66)
Tulsa, OK
918-382-7866 myspace.com/bluedomediner
American – upscale diner food – good – inexpensive –
B&L Sun. thru Tues.; B, L&D Wed.-Sat. – no smoking –
major cards

The Right Wing
3420 E. 11th St. (Route 66)
Tulsa, OK
918-838-9464
American – hot wings – exceptional – inexpensive – L&D
Mon. thru Sat. – no smoking – beer – try the nitro wings –
Visa, MC

Wilson's BBQ
3616 E. 11th St. (Route 66)
Tulsa, OK
918-836-7020
www.wilsonsbar-b-que.com
barbecue – soul food – good – moderate – L&D – 7 days –
open until 10 p.m. – no smoking – beer – major cards –
motto is "You need no teeth to eat our beef"

Tally's Cafe
1102 S. Yale (Route 66)
Tulsa, OK
918-835-8039
American – roast beef, exceptional cinnamon rolls,
barbecue – good – inexpensive – B, L&D – 7 days – no
smoking – great neon sign – major cards

Tacos Fiesta Mexicana
Lewis and 11th Street (Route 66)
Tulsa, OK
918-638-6437
Mexican – authentic Mexican tacos – exceptional –
inexpensive – friendly service – L Mon.; L&D Tue. thru
Sat. – classic "taco truck" – outdoor seating only – try the
lengua tacos – no cards

Billy Ray's BBQ
3524 Southwest Blvd. (Route 66)
Tulsa, OK
918-445-0972
American – barbecue and catfish – good – moderate – L&D
Tue. thru Sat. – no smoking – beer – major cards

Ollie's Station Restaurant ☆
4070 Southwest Blvd. (Route 66)
Tulsa, OK
446-0524 www.olliesstation.com
American – fried chicken – good – a special "must-stop" –
atmosphere – B, L&D Mon.-Sat., B&L Sun. – salad bar –
no smoking – strong Route 66 supporters – dining room is
decorated in a train theme, with model trains running on
tracks suspended from the ceiling – major cards

Hickory House BBQ
626 N. Mission St. (Route 66)
Sapulpa, OK
918-224-7830
www.hickoryhouse66.com
American – barbecue – good – moderate – L&D – closed
Sun. – salad bar – no smoking – beer – Visa, MC, Amex,
Disc

Happy Burger
215 N. Mission (Route 66)
Sapulpa, OK
918-224-7750
American – burgers and fries – good – inexpensive –
L&D Mon. thru Fri., 11 a.m.-4 p.m. Sat. – no smoking –
major cards

Anchor Inn
630 S. Roland St. (Route 66)
Bristow, OK
918-367-9014
American – burgers – good – L&D Tue. thru Sat. – no
smoking – no cards – since 1950

Rock Café ☆
114 W. Main St. (Route 66)
Stroud, OK
918-968-3990
American, German, eclectic – exceptional – try the
jaegerschnitzle and spaetzle – a special "must-stop" –
moderate – B, L&D 7 days – no smoking – restored after a
devastating 2008 fire – owner was the inspiration for Sally
Carrera in the movie "Cars" – major cards

Dan's Bar-B-Que Pit
706 Broadway (Route 66)
Davenport, OK
918-377-2288
barbecue – good – moderate – B, L&D daily – B&L only
Sun. – salad bar Thurs. thru Sun. – no smoking – Visa, MC

Garwooly's
1023 Broadway
(Route 66)
Davenport, OK
918-377-2230
American – Indian tacos, chicken-fried steak – good –
moderate – L&D daily – L only Sun. – no smoking – Visa,
MC, Disc

Early Bird Café
615 Broadway
(Route 66)
Davenport, OK
918-377-2209
American and Mexican – good – inexpensive – try the
dulce de tres leches cake – B, L&D Mon. thru Sat.; B&L
Sun. – no smoking – located in a restored gas station on
Route 66 - major cards

Marsha's Country Kitchen
(formerly Granny's Country Kitchen)
917 Manvel
(Route 66)
Chandler, OK
405-258-2382
American – good – moderate – known for chicken-fried
steak – B, L & D Tue. thru Sat.; B&L only Sun. – no
smoking – no cards

The Boundary on Route 66
16001 E. Hwy. 66
Luther, OK
(405) 277-3532
barbecue – exceptional – value – inexpensive – excellent
ribs, pulled pork – beer – L&D Th. thru Sun. – Visa, MC

POPS ☆
660 W. Hwy. 66
Arcadia, OK
405-928-7677 or 877-266-POPS
www.pops66.com
American – upscale diner food – over 500 kinds of soda –
good – a special "must-stop" – B, L&D – 7 days – no
smoking – great milkshakes – 66-foot-tall neon soda bottle
out front – major cards

Section 9 - Oklahoma City, OK to the outskirts of Clinton, OK.

Lodging:

Lincoln Inn Express Hotel & Suites
5405 N. Lincoln Blvd. (Route 66)
Oklahoma City, OK
405-528-7563
http://lincolninnokc.com/
good - $65-$99 – pool – pets – microwaves & fridges –
nonsmoking rooms – full breakfast – wi-fi internet – laundry –
in-room coffee – irons & boards – blow-dryers – newly
remodeled – patios overlook pool – major cards

Courtyard Marriott
1515 NW Expressway (Temporary Route 66: 1954-55)
Oklahoma City, OK
405-848-0808
www.marriott.com/hotels/travel/okcnw-courtyard-oklahoma-city-northwest
exceptional - $89-$109 – indoor pool – fitness center - free
hi-speed internet – mini fridge & coffee maker – restaurant
(breakfast only) – pets ok with non-refundable fee – all nonsmoking - food and shopping nearby – AAA & Senior rates -
major cards

Holiday Inn Express Hotel & Suites
7840 NW 39th Expressway (Route 66)
Bethany, OK
405.787.6262
www.hiexpress.com/bethany
exceptional - $99-$129 – indoor pool – hot breakfast included
w/room - wi-fi – suites have microwaves & fridges - all
non-smoking - laundry – AAA & AARP discount - fitness
center - major cards

Best Western Mark Motor Hotel
525 E. Main Street (Route 66)
Weatherford, OK
580.772.3325
www.bestwestern.com
exceptional - $80 - $170 – hot breakfast included w/room
outdoor pool - all rooms have microwaves & fridges - wi-fi –
smoking available - AAA & AARP discount - major cards

Dining:

Cheever's Café
2409 N. Hudson
(block off 23rd Street (Route 66: 1926-54)
Oklahoma City, OK
405.525.7007
www.cheeverscafe.com
lunch Mon thru Fri 11am-4pm – dinner Mon thru Thu 4-9:30pm,
Fri 4 thru 10:30pm, Sat 5 thru 10:30pm, Sun brunch 10:30am thru
3:00pm – wine & beer – moderate to expensive - smoking on
outdoor patio - American food w/Southwestern flavor – terrific
restaurant located in a great historic building from the 1920's –
major cards

Big Truck Tacos
530 NW 23rd Street (Route 66: 1926-54)
Oklahoma City, OK
405-525-8226 www.bigtrucktacos.com
seasonal hours (call ahead of time) – B, L & D - non-smoking –
beer – Mexican Coca-Cola – inexpensive - terrific & innovative
Mexican food – voted best new restaurant in OKC 2010 -
major cards

Barry's Grill
3124 N May Ave (Route 66: 1933-54)
Oklahoma City, OK
405-948-7878 www.barrysoldfashioned.com
Mon thru Fri 10:30am-8pm, Sat 11am-6pm, closed Sun –
inexpensive – L&D - no smoking – carry out available – good
thin patty style hamburgers – hand cut fries – great tater tots –
MC, Visa, Disc

Johnnie's Charcoal Broiler
2652 W. Britton Road (Beltline Route 66: 1947-53)
Oklahoma City, OK
405.751.2565 www.johnniesok.com
American - daily 11 am-10 pm – walk up carryout available -
wi-fi - inexpensive - kids menu – no smoking - OKC institution -
best hamburgers and onion rings in the city - also
frankfurters, salads, homemade pies - major cards

VZD's Restaurant & Club ☆

4200 N. Western (1930's Beltline Route 66)
Oklahoma City, OK
405.524.4203 www.vzds.com
American - Mon thru Thur 10:30 am-12 am, Fri & Sat 10:30 am-2 am – closed Sun. – full bar - live music – inexpensive – no smoking award winning burgers - OKC's favorite neighborhood bar, grill & music venue for over 30 years – a must-stop – located in the historic 1920's Veazey drug store - major cards

Ann's Chicken Fry House

4106 NW 39th (Route 66)
Oklahoma City, OK
405-943-8915
American – chicken-fried steak – fried olives – good – moderate – atmosphere – L&D – Tues thru Sat 11 am-8:30 pm closed Sun. & Mon. – no smoking – fun·1950s décor – no cards

Bad Brad's Bar-B-Q Joint

700 W. Main St. (Route 66)
Yukon
405.354.2122 www.badbrads.com
Barbecue - Mon-Thur 11am-8:30pm, Fri & Sat 11 am – 9 pm closed Sun - no smoking – moderate - slow cooked BBQ - they use post oak and pecan for their fire not coal or mesquite - meats are trimmed and hand-cut upon ordering, never pre-cut - sides prepared fresh daily - Visa, MC

Robert's Grill ☆

300 S. Bickford (Route 66)
El Reno, OK
405-262-1262
American – onion burgers and Coney dogs – exceptional – a special "must-stop" – inexpensive – atmosphere – no smoking - a classic counter diner since 1926 – B, L&D 7 days, Mon thru Sat 6 am-9 pm, Sun 6 am-7 pm – no cards

Johnnie's Grill ☆
301 S. Rock Island Avenue (Route 66)
Yukon, OK
(405) 262-4721
Mon thru Sat 6am-9pm, Sun 11am-8pm - American –
exceptional - a special "must-stop" – inexpensive - no smoking -
terrific onion burger and breakfasts – no cards

Jerry's Restaurant
1000 E. Main St.
(Route 66)
Weatherford, OK
580-772-3707
American – chicken-fried steaks and breakfasts – good –
inexpensive – B, L&D 7 days – 24 hours – no smoking – since
1966 – major cards

Lucille's Roadhouse
1301 N. Airport Road
Weatherford, OK
580-772-8808
American – good chicken fried steak &grilled salmon –
moderate – atmosphere – B, L & D Mon thru Sat 6 am-10 pm,
Sun 11am - 2 pm – smoking section with separate ventilation
system – lounge & steak house (alcohol available) open Mon
thru Sat 11am-10pm - gift shop - major cards

Section 10 - Clinton, OK to the outskirts of Shamrock, TX.
Lodging:

Midtown Travel Inn
1015 Gary Blvd. (Route 66)
Clinton, OK
580-323-2466
good - $40-$55 - dining - Cont. breakfast - nonsmoking rooms - pool - internet connections - major cards

Super 8 Motel
1120 South 10th
Clinton, OK
580-323-4979 www.super8.com
good - $45-$65 - Cont. breakfast - nonsmoking rooms - internet connections - ironing boards, hair dryers, senior citizens discounts - major cards

Days Inn
1200 South 10th
Clinton, OK
580-323-5550 www.daysinn.com
good - $69-$125 - full breakfast - dining at the "Branding Iron" - pool - pets - fridges & microwaves - internet connections - nonsmoking rooms - fitness room - major cards

Ramada Inn
2140 Gary Blvd. (Route 66)
Clinton, OK
580-323-2010
www.ramada.com
good - $57.95-$75 - full breakfast - Country Kitchen Restraurant - Hideout Bar - pool - pets - some fridges & microwaves - nonsmoking rooms - internet connections - irons & boards - fitness room - major cards

Budget Inn
2247 Gary Blvd. (Route 66)
Clinton, OK
580-323-6840
good - $39.95-$59.99 - pool - pets - internet connections - major cards

America's Best Value Inn
2015A West 3rd (Route 66)
Elk City
580-243-2103 americasbestvalueinn.com
good - $45-$80 - pets - nonsmoking rooms - internet connections - major cards

Best Western Elk City Inn
2015 West 3rd (Route 66)
Elk City, OK
580-225-2331 www.bestwestern.com
exceptional - $80-$109 - indoor pool - Cont. breakfast - nonsmoking rooms - hair dryers & irons in rooms - internet connections - major cards

Flamingo Inn
2000 W. 3rd (Route 66)
Elk City, OK
580-225-1811
good - $40-$90 - dining - pets - nonsmoking rooms - internet connections - king sized beds available - major cards

Ramada Inn
102 B J Hughes Access Rd.
(I-40 & SH 6)
Elk City, OK
580-225-8140 www.ramada.com
good - $60-$90 - dining - full breakfast - indoor pool - pets - nonsmoking rooms - internet connections - safes in rooms - major cards

AmericInn
2405 S. El Camino (Route 66 exit I-40)
Sayre, OK
580-928-2711 www.americinn.com
good - $74.90-$149.90 - indoor pool - pets - fridges & microwaves - nonsmoking rooms - Cont. breakfast - beer & wine pub - laundry - internet connections - major cards

Premier Inn & Suites
1001 N. Sheb Wooley (SH 30 (Route 66) at I-40)
Erick, OK
580-526-8124
good - $83.99-$110.99 - pets - Cont. breakfast - nonsmoking
rooms - indoor pool - hot tub - major cards

Dining:

Branding Iron
1200 S. 10th St. (In the Days Inn)
Clinton, OK
580-323-5550
American - good - seafood & steaks - salad bar - moderate -
liquor - B, L&D 7 days - no smoking - major cards

Wong's
712 Opal (old Route 66 truck route)
Clinton, OK
580-323-4588
Chinese, American - good - salad bar - moderate - beer & wine -
no smoking - L&D closed Monday - Visa, MC, Disc

Pedro's Mexican Food
123 Avant
Clinton, OK
580-323-2944
Mexican - fajitas, steaks, seafood - good - moderate - L&D 7
days - no smoking - major cards

Adamo's Route 66 Italian Villa ☆
2132 Gary Blvd. (Route 66)
Clinton, OK
580-323-5900
Italian - neopolitan pizza - exceptional - moderate - atmosphere -
service - beer & wine - L&D closed Mon. - no smoking - across
from the Oklahoma Route 66 Museum - major cards

White Dog Hill
22901 Route 66 North
Clinton, OK
580-323-6922
American - choice aged steaks, grilled shrimp, stuffed Cornish
Game Hens, sweet glazed salmon, grilled chicken tequilla, lime
sandwich - exceptional - moderate - atmosphere - service - D
Wed. thru Sat. - no smoking - liquor - historic setting - Visa, MC

Dairy Best
301 S. 19th (19th & Gary Blvd.)
Clinton, OK
580-323-9843
American - hamburgers, broasted chicken, ice cream treats -
good - inexpensive - value - atmosphere - L&D Mon. thru Fri. -
in business in this location since 1960 - Visa & MC on purchases
of $5 and over

The Country Dove ☆
610 W. Third (Route 66)
Elk City, OK
580-225-7028
American - exceptional - chicken/avocado sandwich on a
croissant, famous for "French Silk Pie" - a special "must stop" –
atmosphere - service - moderate - L closed Sunday - nice gift
shop - no smoking - major cards

Lupe's
905 N. Main
Elk City, OK
580-225-7190
Mexican, American - steak, seafood, chili rellenos, fajitas -
exceptional - moderate - atmosphere - service - L&D closed
Sun. - liquor - no smoking - major cards

Golden China
101 Janet's Way
Elk City, OK
580-225-5888
American, Chinese - good - moderate - L&D 7 days - no
smoking - Visa, MC, Disc

Section 11 - Shamrock, TX to the outskirts of Amarillo, TX.

Lodging:

Irish Inn
301 I-40 East
Shamrock, TX
806-256-2106 toll free, reservations 800-538-6747 - exceptional -
$74 up - pool - pets - nonsmoking rooms - microwaves -
laundry - internet in the lobby - major cards

Best Western Shamrock Inn & Suites
1802 N. Main St. (Route 66)
Shamrock, TX
806-256-1001
good - $90 up - pool - spa - Cont. breakfast - laundry - small pets
$10 a day - handicapped rooms - king beds available - major cards

Sleep Inn & Suites
111 E. 15th St.
Shamrock, TX
806-256-2227
www.choicehotels.com
exceptional - $100 up - Cont. breakfast - pool - full kitchens - coffe makers in rooms - nonsmoking rooms - internet connections in rooms - laundry - fitness room - LCD 32" flat screen TVs - safe deposit boxes -major cards

Holiday Inn Express Hotel & Suites - Shamrock North
101 E. 13th St.
Shamrock, TX
806-256-5022
exceptional - $90 up - Cont. breakfast - microwave - indoor pool - pets under 25 lbs. $25, over 25 lbs. $50 - handicap facilities available - safe deposit at front desk - internet connections in rooms laundry - free round of golf at the Shamrock Country Club during your stay - major cards

Blarney Inn - Budget Host
402 E. 12th
Shamrock, TX
806-256-2101 www.budgethost.com
exceptional - $25 up - microwave in storage room - pets with $3 deposit - Cont. Breakfast - cable - nonsmoking rooms -

Cactus Inn
Route 66 Bus. I-40
McLean, TX
806-779-2346
good- $40-$50 - children are free - small pets - microwaves - nonsmoking rooms - internet connections - free coffee & donuts - major cards

Chalet Inn
Exit 113 off I 40
Groom, TX
806-248-7524
good - $39.59 up - small pets - free coffee - nonsmoking rooms - major cards

Budget Host
I-40 and Hwy. 207
Conway, TX
806-537-5111www.budgethost.com
good - $35-$50 - pets - full breakfast - nonsmoking rooms - next
door to Rose's restaurant - major cards

Dining:

Mitchell's Family Restaurant
I-40 East and Highway 183
Shamrock, TX
806-256-2141
American - great chicken fried steak $8.75, seniors $6.75, includes
salad bar - exceptional - moderate - atmosphere - service - BL&D
7 days, opens at 5 AM - salad bar - smoking section - major cards

Hasty's Hamburgers
203 E. 18th St.
Shamrock, TX
806-256-3061
American - hamburgers & fries, ice cream treats - exceptional -
value - moderate - L&D 7 days - family owned - major cards

Red River Steak House ☆
Old 66 Westbound
(101 W, Hwy. 101)
McLean, TX
806-779-8940
American - Fri. ribs & sausage, Sat. prime rib, kabobs, seafood -
salad bar - exceptional - moderate - value - service - a special
"must Stop" - L&D Tues. thry Sat. 11AM - 9 PM - no smoking -
major cards

Big Vern's Steakhouse
200 E. 12th (Route 66)
Shamrock, TX
806-256-2088
American - real Texas steak - exceptional - value - moderate -
atmosphere - service - salad bar - L&D Sun. thru Fri. 11:30 AM -
10PM, Sat. 5PM - 10PM - major cards

Rose's Restaurant
I-40 East Exit 96 .
Conway, TX
806-537-3999
American - specials every week - good - moderate - B,L&D 7
days - no smoking - next door to Budget Host - Visa, MC

Section 12 - Amarillo, TX to the outskirts of Tucumcari, NM.

Lodging:

Holiday Inn
1911 I-40 East (Exit 71)
Amarillo, TX
806-372-8741
www.amarillohi.com
good - $99-$119 - dining - indoor pool - pets - microwaves and
fridges - nonsmoking rooms - complimentary wi-fi - video
arcade & billiards - laundry - major cards

The Big Texan Motel
7701 I-40 East (Exit 75)
Amarillo, TX
800-657-7177
www.bigtexan.com
exceptional - $45.99-$85 - dining at the famous Big Texan Steak
Ranch - motel guests get $2 off breakfast buffet in the Steak
Ranch - Texas-shaped outdoor swimming pool - pets -
nonsmoking rooms - laundry - unusual Old West theme - strong
Route 66 supporters - coffee in rooms - major cards

Hampton Inn
1700 I-40 East (Ross exit)
Amarillo, TX
806-372-1425
www.hamptoninn.com
exceptional - $99-$114 (rates lower Sept. thru May) - pool - pets - nonsmoking rooms - full breakfast - room key gets guests into local gym - irons & boards, hair dryers, coffee, video games in rooms - free local phone calls - lap desks in rooms - manager's reception on Tuesday and Wednesday nights offers complimentary snacks, beer, wine and soda - major cards

Best Western Country Inn
1800 W. Vega Blvd. (Route 66)
Vega, TX
806-267-2131
www.best western.com
good - $69-$89 - pool - pets $10 - fridges - Cont. - internet connections - breakfast - nonsmoking rooms - truck parking - major cards

Bonanza Motel
607 Vega Blvd. (Route 66)
Vega, TX
806-267-2128
value - $35-$45 - pets $5 deposit - microwaves & fridges - nonsmoking rooms - internet connections - major cards

Dining:

Big Texan Steak Ranch ☆
7701 I-40 East Exit 75)
Amarillo, TX
806-372-6000
www.bigtexan.com
American - steaks - exceptional - very special "must sop" - old West atmosphere and decor - moderate - service - if you can eat their 72 oz. steak dinner in one hour, you'll get it free - liquor - B, L&D 7 days - a Texas experience highly rated by national magazines and TV shows - smoking - strong Route 66 supporters - unique gift shop -Wi-Fi hot spot - major cards

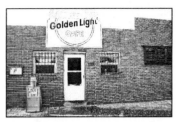

The Golden Light Cafe ☆
209 W. 6th St.
(Route 66)
Amarillo, TX
806-374-9237
goldenlightcafe.com
American - burgers, chili, green chili stew - exceptional - a very special "must stop" - inexpensive - atmosphere - service - smoking - L&D Mon. thru Sat. - beer & wine - est. 1946, said to be the oldest restaurant in Amarillo continouosly operating at the same location on Route 66 - Visa, MC

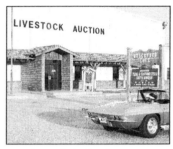

Stockyard Cafe ☆
101 S. Manhattan
Amarillo, TX
806-342-9411
Southwestern/American - chicken fry - exceptional - a special "must stop" - value - service - B&L Mon thry Sat - moderate - located in the big sale barn in the heart of the vast Amarillo stockyards, where several thousand head of beef cattle are auctioned every week - the TV show, "Man Vs Food" was here - major cards

Boot Hill Saloon & Grill
909 Vega Blvd.
Vega, TX
806-267-2904 www.boothillvega.com
American - steak, green chili chicken wontons, jalapeno bacon
wrapped shrimp, fish, ribs - exceptional - moderate -
atmosphere - service - L&D 7 days - liquor - smoking - owned by
Food Network personality Rory Schepisi - Visa, MC, Amex

Smokey Joe's Texas Cafe ☆
2903 SW 6th Ave.
Amarillo, TX
806-331-6698
American - the jalepeno chicken fried steak is exceptional -
L&D - center cut steaks & burgers - service - atmosphere -
a special "must stop" - liquor - major cards

Wild Bill's Fill' N Station ☆
3514 W. 6th Ave.
Amarillo, TX
806-372-4500
American - burgers, chicken fried steak - exceptional - value -
service - atmosphere - a special "must stop" - L&D Mon thru Sat,
B Sat & Sun - beer & wine - major cards

MidPoint Cafe ☆
Route 66
(on the west end of town)
Adrian, TX
806-538-6379
www.midpointroute66cafe.com
American - known for Joann's "Ugly Crust" pies - exceptional -
a special "must stop" - value - atmosphere - service - B&L 7 days,
can take groups for dinner if a reservation is made - moderate -
very friendly - no smoking - strong Route 66 supporters -
landmark, Adrian is considered to be midway between Chicago
and LA on Route 66 - free "Midpoint" bumper stickers - bus, car
& tours welcome - while there, sign Fran's pickup truck named
"Gus" - Visa, MC

Section 13 - Tucumcari, NM to the outskirts of Santa Rosa, NM.

Lodging:

Blue Swallow Motel ☆
815 E. Route 66 Blvd.
Tucumcari, NM
505-461-9849
Toll free 866-461-9849
www.blueswallowmotel.com
exceptional - $69-$129 - This is one of the most popular
properties on 66, so it's a good idea to make advance
reservations. Open only in early spring and summer months - a
very special "must stop" - nonsmoking rooms - morning coffee
in lobby - microwaves & fridges - gift shop - pets, check for
availability - carports - famous neon sign - internet connections
in rooms - beautifully restored mid 30s icon - Visa, MC, Amex

Motel Safari
722 E. Route 66 Blvd.
Tucumcari, NM
575-461-1048
www.smalltown-america.com
exceptional - $69-$119 - nonsmoking rooms - internet
connections in rooms and coffee makers - luxury bath amenities -
newer electronics - 32" HDTVs - nicely renovated - in the heart
of Tucumcari - can reserve online - major cards

Route 66 Motel
1620 E Route 66 Blvd.
Tucumcari, NM
575-461-1212
www.rte66motel.com
good - $30-$$60 - nonsmoking rooms = internet connections in
rooms - a very basic motel that is a nice place to rest your head -
Visa, MC

Travelodge Tucumcari
1214 E. Tucumcari Blvd. (Route 66)
Tucumcari, NM
575-461-1401
good - $69-$109 - Cont. breakfast - pets - nonsmoking rooms -
internet connections, coffee makers, hair dryers in rooms - newly
renovated rooms - classic lodge style mptel - ample RV and truck
parking - major cards

Pow Wow Inn
801 W. Route 66 Blvd.
Tucumcari, NM
575-461-0500
good - $69-$119 - full breakfast - dining - pool - microwaves -
laundry - internet connections, coffee makers, hair dryers in
rooms - restaurant & lounge attached - gift shop - good
proximity to the convention center - still a nice stay for the price -
major cards

Dining:

☞ *New Mexico does not allow smoking in indoor restaurants. If an
establishment has an outdoor patio, it can choose to allow smoking.*

Kix on 66
1102 E. Route 66 Blvd
Tucumcari, NM
575-461-1966
www.kixon66.com
American diner food - breakfast - Seattle's Best Coffee -
exceptional - value - service - B&L 7 days - wi-fi - major cards

Del's Restaurant ☆
1202 E. Route 66 Blvd.
Tucumcari, NM
505-461-1740 www.delsrestaurant.com
American/Mexican - great salad bar - exceptional - a very special
"must stop" - moderate - service - atmosphere - B, L&D Mon.
thru Sat. - soup & salad bar - no smoking - carry out available -
major cards

Lena's
112 E. Main
American/Mexican - solid fare - good - inexpensive - value - B,
L&D Mon. thru Sat. - in downtown Tucumcari - hits the spot for
solid Mexican food - Visa, MC

Rubee's Diner
605 W. Route 66 Blvd.
Tucumcari, NM
505-461-1463
American/Mexican - breakfast burritos - exceptional - service -
B, L&D Mon. thru Sat. - quick & hearty - Visa, MC

Section 14 - Santa Rosa, NM to the outskirts of Albuquerque, NM.

Lodging:

Hampton Inn
2475 Historic Route 66
Santa Rosa, NM
575-472-2300 www.hamptoninn.com
good - $89-$120 - full breakfast - internet connections & coffee makers in rooms - pool - laundry - elevators - business center - hot tub - game room - 100% nonsmoking - major cards

Quality Inn
2533 Historic Route 66 (I-40 exit 277)
Santa Rosa, NM
575-472-5570 & 877-424-6423 www.qualityinn.com
good - $59-$65 - Cont. breakfast - pool - pets $10 - mictowaves & fridges - high speed internet & coffee makers in rooms - wireless in common area - hot tub - RV parking - close to the Blue Hole & Route 66 Auto Museum - major cards

Holiday Inn Express
2516 Historic Route 66 (I-40 exit 277)
Santa Rosa, NM
575-472-5411 www.hiexpress.com
good - $80-$100 - full breakfast - pool - pets $25 - microwaves & fridges - high speed internet connections & coffee makers in rooms - business center - fitness center - RV parking - major cards

Super 8
1611 W. Old Route 66 (I-40 Exit 194)
Moriarity, NM
505-832-6730 www.super8.moriarity.com
good - $$55-$88 - Cont. breakfast - pets $10 - some fridges - RV parking in back - high speed internet connections - nonsmoking rooms - major cards

86

Comfort Inn
119 Route 66 East (I-40 Exit 196)
877-424-6423 www.comfortinn.com
good - $69-$94 - Cont. breakfast - pool - pets - some microwaves
& fridges - high speed internet connections & coffee makers in
rooms - RV parking - major cards

Dining:

☞ *New Mexico does not allow smoking in indoor restaurants. If an
establishment has an outdoor patio, it can choose to allow smoking.*

Comet 2 Drive In Restaurant
217 Historic Route 66
Santa Rosa, NM
505-472-3663
Mexican/American - hamburgers, seafood, homemade pies - fair -
inexpensive - L&D 7 days - no smoking - 3rd generation owners -
strong Route 66 supporters - major cards

Joseph's Bar and Grill
865 Historic Route 66
Santa Rosa, NM
505-472-3361
New Mexican/American - burgers, steaks, catfish - fair - B, L&D
7 days - inexpensive - gift shop - liquor - since 1956 - strong
Route 66 supporters - no smoking - major cards

Silver Moon Cafe
Historic Route 66, east end of town (I-40 Exit 277)
Santa Rosa, NM
505-472-3162
Mexican/American - Santa Fe enciladas - good - B, L&D 7 days - inexpensive - beer - gift shop - strong Route 66 supporters - no smoking - since 1959 - Visa, MC

Clines Corners
One Yacht Club Dr.
Clines Corners, NM
505-472-5488 www.clinescorners.com
American/Southwestern, homemade fudge, also Subway sandwich shop and food court - inexpensive & moderate - good - largest gift shop in NM - strong Route 66 supporters - since 1937 - B, L&D 7 days - salad bar - smoking - major cards

Sun & Sand Restaurant
1124 Historic Route 66
Santa Rosa, NM
505-472-3092
New Mexican/American - fresh cut fries, sopapillas, fresh baked pasteries, root beer floats - inexpensive - good - BL&D 7 days - original Route 66 restaurant dating back over 40 years - show proof of local motel stay (receipt or room key) and get a discount - no credit cards

El Comedor de Anayas
1009 W. Historic Route 66
Moriarity, NM
505-832-4442
Mexican - green chile, Margaritas - good - inexpensive - salad
bar - beer & wine - margaritas - B, L&D 7 days - no smoking -
beer/wine - specials for kids & seniors - major cards

Section 14-A - Santa Rosa, NM up to the outskirts of Santa Fe, NM.

☞ *Las Vegas, NM is the jewel of this early, pre-1937 alignment of
66. It is very picturesque and historic.*

Lodging:

The Historic Plaza Hotel ☆
230 Old Town Plaza
Las Vegas, NM
505-425-3591, 800-328-1882 toll free
www.plazahotel-nm.com
exceptional - a special "must stop" - $69-$199 - kids under 12 with an adult stay free - full breakfast cooked to order - dining - coffee in rooms - some microwaves & fridges - banquet & meeting facilities - pets with $10 deposit - some suites - wireless internet - laundry - nonsmoking rooms - Victorian landmark in historic shopping district known as "the Belle of the Southwest", opened in 1882 on the Santa Fe Trail - The first reuninon of Teddy Roosevelt's Rough Riders was held here - free food specials and entertainment in the Byron T. Saloon (named after the resident ghost), Doc Holiday shot a man in the saloon for cheating - major cards

Holiday Inn Express & Suites
816 Grand Ave.
Las Vegas, NM
866-538-0187 505-426-8182
www.hiexpress.com
good - $85-$164 - full breakfast - indoor pool - pets $15 - some microwaves, fridges & kitchens - nonsmoking rooms - laundry - internet connections & coffee makers in rooms - hot tub - fitness center & business center - major cards

Dining:

☞ *New Mexico does not allow smoking in indoor restaurants. If an establishment has an outdoor patio, it can choose to allow smoking.*

The Plaza Hotel's Landmark Grill
230 Old Town Plaza (in the Hotel)
Las Vegas, NM
505-425-3591, 800-328-1882 toll free
www.plazahotel-nm.com
Mexican/American - char broiled steaks & shops, New Mexican cuisine - good - Early Western Victorian style - moderate - liquor - B, L&D 7 days - live music at dinner - no smoking - major cards

Hillcrest Restaurant
1106 Grand Ave.
Las Vegas, NM
505-425-7211
Mexican/American - steaks, seafood, burgers, ask about the
"Hermit's Peak" - good - inexpensive - BL&D 7 days - liquor -
since 1949 - original 50s juke box - major cards

Estella's Cafe
148 Bridge St.
Las Vegas, NM
505-454-0048
American/New Mexican - chile relenos - good - B, L&D 7 days -
looks like a hole in the wall but worth going in - no smoking -
no credit cards

Section 14B - Santa Fe, NM down to the outskirts of Albuquerque, NM.

Lodging:

☞ *The "Santa Fe Loop" is well worth the extra time it takes. Santa Fe is a very picturesque and historic town. Our adopter has included facilities that are exceptional if you would like to splurge, as well as some lower priced choices.*

Stagecoach Motor Inn
3360 Cerillos Blvd.
(Route 66)
Santa Fe, NM
505-471-0707
good - value - $79-$150 - charming, renovated vintage 1930s inn - 14 rooms including 3 suites (or casitas) - some fireplaces - microwaves & fridges - internet connections in rooms - one suite has a full kitchen - nonsmoking rooms - major cards

Best Western Inn of Santa Fe
3650 Cerrillos Rd.
(Route 66)
Santa Fe, NM
505-438-3822
www.bwsantafehotel.com
good - $89-$149 - Cont. breakfast - value - pool - pets -
microwaves & fridges - suites have full kitchens - family suites (4
beds) & Jacuzzi suites - all nonsmoking rooms - internet
connections in rooms - laundry room - fitness room - newly
renovated rooms - Southwest decor - friendly, helpful staff -
major cards

El Rey Inn ☆
1862 Cerrillos Rd.
(Route 66)
Santa Fe, NM
800-521-1349
www.elreyinnsantafe.com
exceptional - $99-$175 (suites more) - a very special "must stop" -
dining - value - microwaves, fridges & some full kitchens - pool -
pets - Cont. breakfast - nonsmoking rooms - laundry -
microwaves & fridges - internet connection in lobby - whirlpool -
sauna - vintage 66 at its best - beautiful, white adobe-style inn
with authentic Southwestern decor - grounds span 5 acres - some
well-preserved 1936 rooms plus some newer rooms, exquisite
landscaping & gardens, fireplaces, whirlpool, sauna, fitness
center, playground - the El Rey was designed and built by the
same developer as the El Vado Motel on Route 66 in
Albuquerque - major cards

La Fonda Hotel ☆
100 E. San Francisco St.
(Route 66)
Santa Fe, NM
505-982-5511
800-523-5002
www.lafondasantafe.com
exceptional - $219-$339, suites additional - a very special "must stop" - pets - famous - atmosphere - 3 dining rooms - beautiful, historic art deco era, adobe style hotel - unique Southwest art deco style rooms - some private balconies - 24 hr business center - room service - spa & fitness center with hot tub & steam rooms - the open air Bell Tower Bar on the 5th floor overlooks the Santa Fe Plaza - pool - some fireplaces - all nonsmoking rooms - internet connections in rooms - laundry - gift shop - La Fiesta Lounge has live music nightly - major cards

Santa Fe Sage Inn
725 Cerrillos Rd.
(Route 66)
Santa Fe, NM
toll free 866-433-0335
www.santafesageinn.com
good - $75-$160 - value - Cont. breakfast - very professional, helpful staff - pool - pets for a fee - fridges in some rooms - nonsmoking rooms - internet connections in rooms - laundry - 24 hr business center - meeting rooms - excercise room - shuttle service - contemporary, Southwestern style rooms - close to Santa Fe Plaza - major cards

Dining:

☞ *New Mexico does not allow smoking in indoor restaurants. If an establishment has an outdoor patio, it can choose to allow smoking.*

Bobcat Bite ☆
420 Old Las Vegas Hwy. (Route 66)
Santa Fe, NM
505-983-5319 www.bobcatbite.com
American/Western - world famous green chili cheeseburgers, steaks, chops - exceptional - value - atmosphere - moderate - service - a very special "must stop" - established in 1953 - very popular, gets busy, limited seating but worth the wait - original, historic one room, roadside diner - L&D - Wed. thru Sat., Tues. thru Sat. in the summer only - featured in "Hamburger America" as one of the top 100 burgers in the U. S. - beer & wine - no smoking - no cards

Harry's Roadhouse ☆
96B Old Las Vegas Hwy. (Route 66)
Santa Fe, NM
505-989-4629
American/Mexican - value - hearty comfort food - hearty comfort food, lemon ricotta pancakes, meat loaf, sandwiches, burgers & burritos - a very special "must stop" - moderate - exceptional atmosphere - service - value - no smoking - B, L&D 7 days - beer & wine - if they are very busy, for faster seating, ask to eat at the counter or in the bar - also beautiful garden seating - major cards

Café Pasqual's
121 Don Gaspar
Santa Fe, NM
800-722-7672
www.pasquals.com
All organic American/Mexican/Asian artfully prepared -
breakfasts & enchiladas - exceptional - value - moderate - B, L&D
7 days - no smoking - atmosphere - liquor - located near the
Santa Fe Plaza - very popular - owner/chef, Katherine Kagel
published "Cooking with Cafe Pasqual's" - major cards

La Plazuela (in the La Fonda Hotel) ☆
100 E. San Francisco
Santa Fe, NM
505-982-551
800-523-5002 lafondasantafe.com
New Mexican/American - steak, seafood, squash blossoms,
enchiladas - fresh guacamole - award winning culinary team -
exceptional - a very special "must stop" - expensive to
moderate - atmosphere - service - B,L&D 7 days - no smoking -
liquor - enclosed courtyard restaurant in the center of the hotel
with skylights, fountain, famous handpainted glass walls - one
of the most beautiful dining spots in Santa Fe - major cards

Plaza Cafe
54 Lincoln Ave.
Santa Fe, NM
505-952-1664
www.thefamousplazacafe.com
American/New Mexican/Greek - blue corn green chile carne
asada enchiladas, chicken fried steak, moussaka - good -
moderate - B, L&D 7 days - no smoking - beer & wine - historic
location on the plaza - owned by the same family since 1947 -
major cards

Atomic Grill
103 E. Water St.
Santa Fe, NM
505-820-2866
www.theatomicgrill.com
American/New Mexican - fried avacado and crab salad, pizza -
100 varieties of beer - full espresso bar - good - moderate -
B, L&D 7 days - beer & wine - indoor & patio dining on the
plaza - wi-fi available - open late - major cards

The Pantry ☆
1820 Cerrillos Rd.
Santa Fe, NM
505-986-0022
www.thepantrysantafe.com
New Mexican/American - outstanding huevos rancheros -
exceptional - value - a very special "must stop" - inexpensive to
moderate - atmosphere - service - B, L&D 7 days - no smoking - a
true roadside gem - located near the El Rey Motel - friendly
staff - major cards

97

Range Café ☆
925 Camino Del Pueblo
(Route 66)
Bernalillo, NM
505-867-1700
www.rangecafe.com
Western American/Mexican - coconut cream pie, meat loaf,
campfire trout, blue corn enchiladas, said to have the best fish &
chips anywhere - exceptional - a very special "must stop" -
B, L&D 7 days - moderate - service - atmosphere, artful decor -
no smoking - "Home at the Range" gift shop - favorite stop for
66rs - their motto is, "Ordinary food done extraordinarily well."
and it's true - liquor - live music nightly in the bar - major cards

Section 15 - Albuquerque, NM to the outskirts of Grants, NM.

Lodging:

Ambassador Inn
7407 Central Ave. NE
(Route 66)
Albuquerque, NM
505-265-1161
good - $35-$75 - value - suites available - newer facility - small
pets - indoor heated pool & spa - some microwaves & fridges -
Cont. breakfast - nonsmoking rooms - internet connections in
rooms - laundry - major cards

Luxury Inn
6718 Central Ave. SE
(Route 66)
Albuquerque, NM
505-255-5900
888-883-2228
good - $35-$55 - Cont. breakfast - value - heated indoor pool - microwaves & fridges - laundry - spa - major cards

Stardust Inn
801 Central Ave. NE
(Route 66)
Albuquerque, NM
505-243-2891
www.downtownstardustinn.com
good - value - $49-$69 - Cont. breakfast - pool - fridges, microwaves, coffee makers & hair dryers - dogs with a fee - nonsmoking rooms - internet connections - remodeled facility - major cards

The Hotel Blue
717 Central Ave. NW
(Route 66)
Albuquerque, NM
505-924-2400
www.thehotelblue.com
good - $69-$149 - pool - pets - deluxe Cont. breakfast - nonsmoking rooms - microwaves & fridges - coffee makers, HDTVs, irons & hair dryers, Tempurpedic beds, wireless internet connections in rooms - exercise room - handicapped accessible rooms - secured parking - business center - free airport - major cards

Monterey Non-smokers Motel ☆
2402 Central Ave. SW
(Route 66)
Albuquerque, NM
505-243-3554
www.nonsmokersmotel.com
exceptional - $58-$90 - value - a very special "must stop" - classic
Route 66 motel in beautiful condition - new room interiors -
outdoor heated pool - fridges, hair dryers & coffee makers in
rooms - all nonsmoking rooms - laundry - wireless internet
connections - computer in lobby for guests - major cards

Sandia Peak Inn
4614 Central Ave. SW
(Route 66)
Albuquerque, NM
505-831-5036
www.sandiapeakinnmotel.com
exceptional - $59-$125 - value - full breakfast - new motel - large
rooms - indoor heated pool - Jacuzzis in the king suites - small
pets - microwaves & fridges - nonsmoking rooms - internet
connections in rooms - laundry - hair dryers, irons - lobby open
24 hrs. - handicapped accessible rooms - major cards

Dining:

☞ *New Mexico does not allow smoking in indoor restaurants. If an
establishment has an outdoor patio, it can choose to allow smoking.*

Loyola's
4500 Central Ave. SE
(Route 66)
Albuquerque, NM
505--268-6478
American/New Mexican - liver & onions, chiles, home made
baked goods - good - atmosphere - service - moderate - B&L
Tues. thru Sun. - since the 1950s - busy local restaurant - very
clean and well maintained - does not allow smoking -
Visa, MC, Disc

La Provence ☆
3001 Central Ave. NE
(Route 66)
Albuquerque, NM
505-254-7644
www.laprovencenobhill.com
French - poultry, seafood, beef quiche, crepes - moderate -
atmosphere - service - exceptional - a very special "must stop" -
L&D 7 days, Sunday brunch - beer & wine - 1930s corner gas
station - patio dining - same owners as Scalo - major cards

Scalo ☆
3500 Central Ave. SE
(Route 66)
Albuquerque, NM
505-255-8781
www.scalonobhill.com
Northern Italian - fresh fish, ravioli, cappelinni - exceptional -
a very special "must stop" - liquor, excellent wine list - patio
dining - atmosphere - service - L&D 7 days - moderate to
expensive - longtime established restaurant in the historic 1947
Nob Hill Shopping Center (on the National Register of Historic
Places) - free parking in back - major cards

Kellys Restaurant & Brew Pub ☆
3222 Central Ave. SE
(Route 66)
Albuquerque, NM
505-262-2739
www.kellysbrewpub.com
American - Albuquerque turkey, buffalo burgers - exceptional -
atmosphere - a very special "must stop" - value - service -
B, L&D 7 days - smoking on patio only - beer & wine - brew their
own beer - moderate to inexpensive - in the 1939 Jones Ford Co.
building (on the National Register of Historic Places) -
major cards

Gruet Steakhouse ☆
3201 Central Ave. SE
(Route 66)
Albuquerque, NM
505-256-9463
www.gruetsteakhouse.com
American - steak, cracklin' pork shank, local sparking wine -
exceptional - atmosphere - a very special "must stop" - service -
D 7 days - expensive - liquor, extensive wine list - located in the
1936 Monte Vista fire station (on the National register of Historic
Places) - major cards

Mannies
2900 Central Ave. SE (Route 66)
Albuquerque, NM
505-265-1669
American - diner road food - good - inexpensive - value - large,
bustling, well established - B, L & D 7 days - breakfast all day -
near University of NM - everything is home made - smoking on
patio only - major cards

Route 66 Diner
1405 Central Ave. NE
(Route 66)
Albuquerque, NM
(505) 247-1421
www.66diner.com
American - diner food and decor - green chile hamburgers,
stew - souvenirs - Route 66 "Pile Up" - good - L&D 7 days, B Sat.
& Sun. - inexpensive - atmosphere - value - beer & wine - strong
Route 66 supporters - major cards

Artichoke Cafe ☆
424 Central Ave. SE
(Route 66)
Albuquerque, NM
505-243-0200
New American - Niman Ranch organic meats, fresh fish,
vegetarian dishes - exceptional - a very special "must stop" -
moderate to expensive - value - atmosphere - service - L&D 7
days - beer & wine - happy hour Mon. thru Fri. 3 to 6 pm - new
lounge area - historic retail block - attended secure parking -
major cards

Standard Diner ☆
320 Central Ave. SE
(Route 66)
Albuquerque, NM
505-243-1440
www.standarddiner.com
eclectic upscale diner food - home made breads & desserts -
exceptional - value - a very special "must stop"- moderate -
atmosphere - service - new conversion of a 1938 Carothers &
Mauldin service station - L&D 7 days, Sun. brunch 9 am to
3 pm - friendly staff - featured on TV's "Diners, Drive Ins &
Dives" - major cards

Nick's Crossroads Cafe
400 Central Ave. SW
(Route 66)
Albuquerque, NM
505-242-8369
Greek American - gyros, salads - good - value - inexpensive -
atmosphere - service - B&L 7days - major cards

Fresh Choices
402 Central Ave. SW
(Route 66)
Albuquerque, NM
505-242-6447
Italian buffet - home style breads & sauces - good - value - L&D
Mon. thru Sat. - salad bar - inexpensive - beer & wine -
atmosphere - service - quiet place in bustling downtown -
friendly staff - major cards

Lindy's
500 Central Ave. SW
 (Route 66)
Albuquerque, NM
505-242-2582
American diner food - also Mexican & Greek - extensive menu -
blue plate special, steaks, espresso - exceptional - est. 1929 -
atmosphere, nice diner decor - service - B, L&D 7 days, breakfast
all day - inexpensive - beer & wine - in the heart of downtown -
Visa, MC

Duran Central Pharmacy
1815 Central Ave. NW (Route 66)
Albuquerque, NM
505-247-4141
New Mexican - green & red chile - exceptional - value -
moderate - B, L&D Mon. thru Sat. - longtime local hangout -
no cards

Western View Diner
6411 Central Ave. NW (Route 66)
Albuquerque, NM
(505) 836-2200
American & Mexican - steak - good - value - inexpensive -
atmosphere - service - B, L&D 7 days , no dinner on Sun. -
beer & wine - Route 66 institution since 1940's - major cards

Section 15A - From Albuquerque, NM to the outskirts of Mesita, NM

☞ *This little known, historic section is becoming increasingly popular with Route 66 travelers because it is well worth the short trip.*

Lodging:

Los Lunas Inn & Suites
1711 Main St. SW (Route 66)
Los Lunas, NM
505-865-5100
exceptional - $60-$100 - deluxe Cont. breakfast - value - heated
pool - small pets - microwaves & fridges - nonsmoking rooms -
internet connections, coffee makers, hair dryers in rooms -
laundry - business center - fitness center - meeting rooms - newly
remodeled - nonsmoking rooms - major cards

Western Skies Inns & Suites
2258 Sun Ranch Village Loop
(I-25 & Hwy. 6 - Route 66)
Los Lunas, NM
505-865-0001
www.westernskiesinnsuites.com
good - $59-$69 - deluxe Cont. breakfast - pool - pets - some
microwaves & fridges - internet connections & coffee makers in
rooms - gift shop - major cards

Dining:

☞ New Mexico does not allow smoking in indoor restaurants. If an establishment has an outdoor patio, it can choose to allow smoking.

El Camino Dining Room
6800 4th St. NW
(Route 66)
Albuquerque, NM
505-344-0448
New Mexican - good - inexpensive - value - atmosphere - service - B&L Tues. thru Sun. - beer & wine - since the 1950s - traditional adobe construction - major cards

Sadie's
6230 4th St. NW
(Route 66)
Albuquerque, NM
505-345-5339 www.sadiesofnewmexico.com
New Mexican - good - moderate - atmosphere - service - L&D 7 days - liquor - large, bustling restaurant opened in the 1950s - popular with locals - major cards

Mr. Powdrell's Original Barbeque
5209 4th St. NW
(Route 66)
Albuquerque, NM
505-345-8086
BBQ - exceptional - value - moderate - service - L&D Tues. thru Sun. - building on the National Register of Historic Places - family business since 1870 - major cards

Mary & Tito's Cafe ☆
2711 4th St. NW (Route 66)
Albuquerque, NM
505-344-6266
New Mexican - carne adovada, red & green chilecombionation stuffed turnovers - exceptional - value - a very special "must stop" - inexpensive - service - atmosphere - B, L&D Mon. thru Sat. - voted best red chile in NM - 2010 James Beard Foundation Award winner - Visa, MC

Original Garcia's Kitchen
1113 4th St. NW
(Route 66)
Albuquerque, NM
505-247-9149
Spanish American - carne adovada. sopapillas - exceptional - value - inexpensive - local chain with 2 other locations on 66 that are also open for dinner - service - B&L 7 days - beer & wine - major cards

Red Ball Cafe ☆
1303 4th St. SW
(Route 66)
Albuquerque, NM
505-247-9498
New Mexican / American - award winning Wimpyburgers, enchilladas, green chile cheeseburgers - good - value - exceptional - a very special "must stop" - inexpensive - atmosphere - service - B&L Tues. thru Sat. - one of Route 66's oldest restaurants - since 1922 - in an old part of Albuquerque (Barallas) nicely restored and maintained (building on the National Register of Historic Places - smoking on patio only - major cards

107

The Luna Mansion ☆
Hwy. 6 & Hwy. 314 (Route 66)
Los Lunas, NM
505-865-7333
American - Mansion Steak, seafood - exceptional - a very special
"must stop" - value - moderate to expensive - service - atmosphere -
D Tues. thru Sun. - liquor - Spirit Lounge on the 3rd floor opens at
3:30 - Southern style stucco mansion on National Register of
Historic Places, dates to 1881 - newly refurbished and upgraded -
property was part of a 1692 land grant - major cards

Section 16 - From Grants, NM to the outskirts of Gallup, NM.

Lodging:

Sands Motel
112 McArthur
Grants, NM
505-287-2996
good - $31-$60 - pets - Cont. breakfast - microwaves & fridges -
nonsmoking rooms - 1/2 block off the route - microwaves &
fridges - Elvis Presley stayed here in 1963 on his way to
Las Vegas to get married. His registration form is framed in
Room 123. - major cards

Days Inn
1504 E. Santa Fe Ave. (Route 66)
Grants, NM
505-287-8883 Fax - 505- 287-7772
www.daysinn.com
good - $40-$90 - Cont. breakfast - pets - microwaves & fridges -
laundry - business fax service - free newspaper - voice mail -
wireless internet connections - nonsmoking rooms - major cards

Best Western
1501 E. Santa Fe Ave. (Route 66)
Grants, NM
505-287-7901www.bestwestern.com
good - $59-$89 - pool - pets - dining - New Mexico Steakhouse 5
pm to 9 pm 7 days - Rookies Sports Bar 4:30 pm to 11 pm 7 days -
nonsmoking rooms - Jacuzzi - fitness room - internet
connections - major cards

South West Motel
1000 E. Santa Fe Ave. (Route 66)
Grants, NM
505-287-2935
good - $29.95-$39.95 - pets - microwaves & fridges - nonsmoking
rooms - internet connections in rooms - HBO - fax service -
major cards

Dining:

☞ *New Mexico does not allow smoking in indoor restaurants. If an establishment has an outdoor patio, it can choose to allow smoking.*

El Cafecito
820 E. Santa Fe Ave.
(Route 66)
Grants, NM
505-285-6229
New Mexican/American - exceptional enchiladas - value - B, L&D Mon. thru Sat. - inexpensive - a new building on the same site with more seating - expanded menu - banquet room - Visa, MC, Disc

1st Street Cafe on Santa Fe
1600 W. Santa Fe Ave.
(Route 66)
Grants, NM
505-287-7111
American/Mexican - sandwiches, home made pies, some vegetarian items, will substitute ingredients to fit dietary requirements - B&L Tues. thru Sun. 7 am to 2 pm, breakfast served all day - major cards

Grants Cafe
932 E. Santa Fe Ave. (Route 66)
Grants, NM
505--285-6474
good - American/New Mexican - home cooking - inexpensive -
service - B&L 6 am to 2 pm Mon. Thru Fri. - since 1950s - neon
sign recently restored - some 66 memorabilia - no smoking - Visa,
MC, Amex

El Ranchero Cafe
609 W. Hwy. 66
Milan, NM
505-876-1032
good - New Mexican - inexpensive - B, L&D 7 days - major cards

Lodging:

El Rancho Hotel & Motel ☆
1000 E. Hwy. 66
Gallup, NM
505-863-9311
www.elranchohotel.com
good - $82-$107 - a very special "must stop" - dining - pool - pets - some fridges - laundry - wi-fi internet connections in common areas - historic Route 66 landmark - gift shop - since 1937 - remarkable lobby with photographs of celebrities who have stayed there while making movies - rooms are named after the celebrities who once stayed in them - nonsmoking rooms - major cards

La Quinta Inn & Suites
3880 E. Hwy 66
Gallup, NM
505-722-2233 www.lq.com
good - $84-$120 - Cont. breakfast - indoor pool - pets - microwaves & fridges - nonsmoking rooms - wi-fi internet connections in rooms - laundry fitness center - major cards

Hampton Inn - Gallup West
11 Twin Buttes Rd. (I-40 exit 16 & Route 66)
Gallup, NM
505-722-7224 www.hampton.com
exceptional - $90-$120 - indoor pool - nonsmoking rooms - full breakfast - internet connections in rooms - fitness room - laundry - the Hampton Inn chain is a strong Route 66 supporter - business center - major cards

Wigwam Motel ☆
811 W. Hopi Dr.
(Route 66)
Holbrook, AZ
928-524-3048 (call after 3 pm MST)
www.wigwamgazette.info
good - $52-$58 - this is one of two historic motels remaining on Route 66 that features wigwam shaped cottages - a very special "must stop" - gift shop - museum - vintage cars & trucks are displayed on the grounds - operated by the same family since the 40s - nonsmoking rooms - no phones in rooms - Visa, MC

America's Best Inns
2211 E. Navajo Blvd.
(Route 66)
Holbrook, AZ
928-524-2654
www.americasbestinns.com
good - value - $45-$51 - Cont. breakfast - pets - nonsmoking rooms - fridges & microwaves - eco-friendly rooms available for people with allergies - wi-fi internet connections - exercise room - major cards

Motel 6
2514 Navajo Blvd.
(Route 66)
Holbrook, AZ
928-524-6101
www.motel6.com
good - $40-$45 - value - pool - pets - nonsmoking rooms - wi-fi internet connections in rooms - microwaves & fridges - laundry - major cards

Dining:

☞ New Mexico does not allow smoking in indoor restaurants. If an establishment has an outdoor patio, it can choose to allow smoking.

Angela's Cafe con Leche
201 E. Hwy. 66
Gallup, NM
505-722-7526
American - coffees - good - value - inexpensive - atmosphere - B&L Mon. & Tues., B&L Wed. thru Fri. - in a renovated Santa Fe depot, now the Gallup Cultural Center - museum, gift shop, historical displays - Visa, MC

Earl's Family Restaurant
1400 E. Hwy. 66
Gallup, NM
505-863-4201
American/Mexican - good - inexpensive -value - B, L&D 7 days - salad bar - native Americans offer crafts to diners - since 1947 - major cards

Jerry's Cafe
406 W. Coal Ave.
(Coal Ave, is one block south of Route 66)
Gallup, NM
505-722-6775
Mexican - exceptional - inexpensive - B, L&D Mon. thru Sat. - Visa, MC

Badlands Grill
2201 W. Hwy. 66
Gallup, NM
505-722-5157
www.badlandsgrill.com
American - steak, fish - exceptional - expensive - service -
D Mon. thru Sat. - liquor - major cards

Route 66 Diner
(I40 exit 339/South on US 191) 1 block East of post office
Sanders, AZ
928-688-2537
American/Mexican - good - value - B, L&D 8 am to 8 pm Mon.
thru Fri. - inexpensive - was an original 1946 Valentine Diner
from Holbrook - Visa, MC

Joe & Aggie's Cafe
120 W. Hopi Dr.
Holbrook, AZ
928-524-6540
Mexican/American - good - value - inexpensive - B, L&D Mon.
thru Fri. - beer & wine - gift shop - since 1943 - Visa, MC

Mesa Italiana Restaurant
2318 E. Navajo Blvd.
Holbrook, AZ
928-524-6696
Italian/American - exceptional - liquor - moderate - L Mon.-Fri.,
D 7 days - major cards

Lodging:

La Posada ☆
303 E. 2nd St. (Route 66)
Winslow, AZ
(928) 289-4366
www.laposada.org
exceptional - $109-$169 - one of America's treasures – beautifully restored Harvey House designed by Mary Jane Coutlter – a very special "must stop" - opened in 1930 - Turquoise Dining Room – lounge - pets – all nonsmoking rooms – coffee service – wireless internet - gift shop - 45 rooms - major cards

Econo Lodge
1706 North Park (off I-40, 1.5 miles north of Route 66)
Winslow, AZ
(928) 289-4687
www.econolodge.com
good - $49-$59 – chain hotel run by pleasant staff – near major stores & dining – adjacent to Mojo Café – outdoor pool – pets - microwaves & fridges - nonsmoking rooms/ smoking rooms available – Cont. breakfast – wireless internet – laundry - 72 rooms - major cards

Best Western Winslow Inn
816 Transcon Lane (off I-40, .5 miles north of Route 66)
Winslow, AZ
(928) 289-2960 www.bestwestern.com
good - $89-$99 – chain hotel slightly off the beaten path –
recently remodeled – indoor pool - $20 deposit for pets –
fridges – microwave in breakfast area – all nonsmoking rooms –
full breakfast – wireless internet - major cards

Best Western Pony Soldier
3030 E. Route 66
Flagstaff, AZ
(928) 526-2388
www.bestwesternponysoldier.com
good - $59-$149 – chain hotel run by efficient staff - enclosed
pool – pets - microwaves & fridges - all nonsmoking rooms –
Cont. breakfast – wireless internet – 75 rooms - major cards

Monte Vista Hotel
100 N. San Francisco St. (just north of Route 66)
Flagstaff, AZ
(928) 779-6971 www.hotelmontevista.com
good - $65-$175 - restored historic hotel – dining & café - lively
cocktail lounge - pets - all nonsmoking rooms – wireless
internet – 42 rooms - major cards

Weatherford Hotel
23 North Leroux
(just north of Route 66)
Flagstaff, AZ
(928)-779-1919
www.weatherfordhotel.com
good - $49-$130 – restored 1897 historic hotel – Charly's Pub and
Grill - lively downtown area - no pets - all nonsmoking - coffee
service – telephones in queen suites only – no room phones –
11 rooms – major cards

Grand Canyon International Hostel
19 1/2 South San Francisco St.
(just south of Route 66)
Flagstaff, AZ
(888) 442-2696
www.grandcanyonhostel.com
exceptional value for budget travelers & backpackers – $38-$45
private room with shared bathroom - $20 dorm (4 persons per
dorm) – Arizona's oldest hostel, open year-round in renovated
1933 building - no pets - 2 kitchens – sinks & fridges in each
room – all nonsmoking rooms - coffee service – Cont. breakfast -
wireless internet – laundry - 8 private & 4 dorm rooms -
major cards

Dubeau Route 66 International Hostel
19 West Phoenix
(early Route 66 alignment just south of Route 66)
Flagstaff, AZ
(800) 398-7112
www.dubeauhostel.com
exceptional value for budget travelers & backpackers – $42-$48
private room & bathroom - $20 dorm (4-8 persons per dorm) –
Arizona's oldest hostel in the original 1929 Dubeau Inn
building - closed Nov.- Mar. - no pets - 2 kitchens - microwaves
& fridges – all nonsmoking rooms - coffee service - Cont.
breakfast - wireless internet – laundry - 11 private & 4 dorm
rooms - major cards

Travel Inn
801W. Route 66
Flagstaff, AZ
(888) 828-4984
www.travelinn66.com
good - $40-$99 – family owned and well run – pets – hot tub –
dry sauna – fridges & microwaves – nonsmoking rooms/
smoking rooms available – Cont. breakfast – wireless internet –
laundry – 48 rooms - major cards

Drury Inn and Suites
300 S. Milton Rd.
(Route 66)
Flagstaff, AZ
(928) 773-4900
www.druryhotels.com
good - $109-$209 – conveniently located chain hotel next to
Northern Arizona University – indoor pool – pets – fridges &
microwaves – all nonsmoking – full breakfast – wireless
internet – fitness center - laundry – 160 rooms – major cards

Radisson Woodlands Hotel
1175 W. Route 66
Flagstaff, AZ
(928) 773-8888 www.flagstaffwoodlandshotel.com
good - $79-$149 – comfortable chain hotel with 2 restaurants –
lounge – indoor pool – whirlpool – no pets - some fridges &
microwaves – all nonsmoking rooms – wireless internet – fitness
center – 183 rooms - major cards

Dining:

☞ *All dining establishments in Arizona are nonsmoking.*

Turquoise Room (in La Posada Hotel) ☆
303 E. 2nd St. (Route 66)
Winslow, AZ
(928) 289-2888 www.theturquoiseroom.net
American Southwestern – Chef John Sharpe serves up an
exceptional experience in this beautifully restored Harvey House
dining room – a very special "must stop" - Martini Lounge -
moderate to expensive - B, L&D 7 days – liquor – major cards

Casa Blanca Café
1201 E. 2nd St. (Route 66)
Winslow, AZ
(928) 289-4191
Authentic Mexican food for over 65 years – exceptional food
prepared from scratch – inexpensive – L&D 7 days – beer &
wine – major cards

Falcon Restaurant
1113 E. 3rd St.
(Route 66)
Winslow, AZ
(928) 289-2628
American – good - original 1950s roadside café inexpensive –
B, L&D 7 days - liquor – lounge attached - major cards

Old Smokey's 2Bar3 Restaurant and Saloon
5877 Leupp Road
(1/4 m. north of Townsend Winona Rd., orig. Route 66
alignment)
Winona, AZ
(928) 522-9260
American – good – roadhouse barbeque cooking - Gateway to
Grand Falls - moderate – L&D, closed Tues. - liquor - lounge –
patio – major cards

Miz Zip's
2924 E. Route 66
Flagstaff, AZ
(928) 526-0104
American – exceptional breakfast place since 1952 – steaks &
burgers - cut their own meat - inexpensive - B, L&D, closed
Sun. – no cards

Grand Canyon Café
10 E. Route 66
Flagstaff, Arizona
(928) 774-2252
American/Chinese – good food served in authentic Route 66
café - chicken fried steak specialty – inexpensive - B, L&D, closed
Sun. - beer/wine - no cards

Mountain Oasis
11 E. Aspen (one block north of Route 66)
Flagstaff, AZ
(928) 214-9270 www. themenuplease.com/mountainoasis
American eclectic – exceptional food & wine list – pasta, fish, &
vegan menu – moderate to expensive – L&D 7 days – liquor –
major cards

Alpine Pizza
7 North Leroux (just north of Route 66)
Flagstaff, AZ
(928) 779-4109
American – good - 30 years a local favorite – small patio -
inexpensive - L&D 7 days – beer & wine – major cards

Beaver Street Brewery and Whistle Stop Cafe
11 S. Beaver St. (just south of Route 66)
Flagstaff, AZ
(928) 779-0079
www.beaverstreetbrewery.com
American – good - first micro-brewery in Flagstaff - lively local
hangout – billiard room - moderate – L&D, closed Mon. –
liquor – seasonal beer garden - major cards

Macy's European Coffeehouse & Bakery ☆
14 S. Beaver St. (just south of Route 66)
Flagstaff, AZ
(928) 774-2243
www.macyscoffee.net
American eclectic – exceptional baked goods & extensive
vegetarian fare served in laid back atmosphere – a very special
"must stop" - roasted coffee beans – photography gallery -
inexpensive - B, L&D 7 days – no cards

Café Ole
119 S. San Francisco St. (south of Route 66)
Flagstaff, AZ
(928) 774-8272
Mexican – exceptional food served in colorful environment –
occasional live music – outdoor tables - moderate - L&D 7 days -
liquor – major cards

Galaxy Diner
931 W. Route 66
Flagstaff, AZ
(928) 774-2466
American – excellent - classic diner food since 1952 - splits, malts
& shakes – weekend entertainment & car shows - inexpensive –
B, L&D 7 days - beer & wine – major cards

Halli's Place
Route 66 at Spring Valley Road
(I-40 exit #178)
Parks, AZ
(928) 635-4741
American deli – good – roadside stop formerly known as Parks in the Pines General store - pizza & sandwiches – original 1906 general store exterior - picnic tables - inexpensive – deli open 7 days - liquor - major cards

Section 19 - Williams, AZ to the outskirts of Hackberry, AZ
Lodging:

Mountain Side Inn & Conference Center
642 E. Route 66
Williams, AZ
800-462-9381 www.mountainsideinngrandcanyon.com
good - $25-$99 - Cont. breakfast - dining - pool - dogs only - microwaves & fridges - nonsmoking rooms - internet connections in rooms - coffee makers, hair dryers, irons & boards - laundry across street - major cards

The Canyon Motel & Railroad RV Park ☆
1900 E. Rodeo Rd. (Route 66)
Williams, AZ
928-635-9371 res 800-482-3955 www.thecanyonmotel.com
exceptional - $44-$160 - a very special "must stop" - pool - pets in
the RV park only - microwaves & fridges - nonsmoking rooms -
laundry - internet connections in rooms - bbqs, fire rings, train
car suites, rooms in 2 cabooses - est. 1948 - Visa, MC, Disc

Route 66 Inn
128 E. Route 66
Williams, AZ
928-635 4791 www.route66inn.com
good - $49-$89 - Cont. breakfast - a few large family suites -
microwaves & fridges - nonsmoking rooms - gift shop - wi-fi
internet connections in rooms - discounts available for some
restaurants - laundry across street - major cards

Best Western Inn of Williams
2600 W. Route 66
Williams, AZ
928-635-4400
exceptional - $129-$189 - full breakfast - pool - pets $25 -
nonsmoking rooms - fridges - microwaves & fridges available -
dining - live entertainment - internet connections in rooms -
laundry - fire pit - lounge - Jacuzzi - major cards

El Rancho Motel
617 E. Route 66
Williams, AZ
928-635-2552
good - $40-$88 - pool - pets in some rooms - microwaves &
fridges - nonsmoking rooms - VCRs, HDTVs coffeemakers,
internet connections in rooms - laundry next door - major cards

The Red Garter ☆
137 W. Railroad Ave. (Route 66)
Williams, AZ
928-635-1484 www.redgarter.com
exceptional Bed & Breakfast - $120-$145 - a very special "must
stop" - dining in the breakfast bakery attached - Cont. breakfast -
all nonsmoking rooms - internet connections in rooms - near the
Grand Canyon Railway station - Visa, MC, Disc

Econo Lodge
302 East Route 66
Williams, AZ
928-635-4085 www.econolodge.com
good - $49-$129 - full breakfast - nonsmoking rooms - coffee
makers, wi-fi internet connections in rooms - microwaves &
fridges - all king & queen beds - redecorated in 2007 - major cards

Highlander Motel
533 W. Route 66
Williams, AZ
928-635-2541 www.highlandermotel.net
good - $50-$65 - Cont. breakfast - microwaves & fridges -
nonsmoking rooms - coffee makers, internet connections in
rooms - major cards

The Lodge On Route 66 ☆
200 E. Route 66   ·
Williams, AZ
928-635-4534 www.thelodgeonroute66.com
exceptional - $79-$189 - Cont. breakfast - a very special "must
stop" - value - microwaves, fridges, whirlpool tubs in some
rooms - nonsmoking rooms - laundry across street - major cards

Rodeway Inn
334 E. Route 66
Williams, AZ
928-635-2619 www.rodewayinn/hotel/az242
good - $39.99-$89.99 - Cont. breakfast - microwaves, fridges,
internet connections in rooms - nonsmoking rooms - major cards

Grand Canyon Hotel ☆
145 W. Route 66
Williams, AZ
928-635-1419 www.thegrandcanyonhotel.com
exceptional - hotel $60-$125, hostel $25 - themed rooms - dining -
value - a very special "must stop" - fridges - nonsmoking
rooms - internet connections in rooms - built in 1891 -
major cards

Canyon Country Inn
442 W. Route 66
Williams, AZ
928-635-2349
good - $64-$97 - Cont. breakfast - microwaves & fridges -
nonsmoking rooms - wi-fi internet connections in rooms -
major cards

Rodeway Inn & Suites - The Downtowner Motel
201 E. Route 66
Williams, AZ
928-635-4041 www.thedowntowneronroute66.com
exceptional - $89-$169 - Cont. breakfast - recently renovated - microwaves & fridges - whirlpool tubs in some rooms - nonsmoking rooms - internet connections - laundry across street - major cards

Historic Route 66 Motel ☆
22750 W. Hwy. 66
Seligman, AZ
928-422-3204 www.route66seligmanarizona.com
good - $45-$57 - a very special "must stop" - internet connections, fridges & coffee makers in rooms - discount at restaurant next door - call for nonsmoking rooms - major cards

Deluxe Inn
22295 Highway 66
928-422-3244
Seligman, AZ
good - $45-$57 - pets - value - microwaves & fridges - nonsmoking rooms - internet connections in rooms - major cards

Supai Motel
22450 Highway 66
Seligman, AZ
928-422-4153
www.supaimotel.com
good - $45-$57 - value - nonsmoking rooms - microwaves &
fridges - internet connections in rooms - recently refurbished -
major cards

Hualapai Lodge
900 Route 66
Peach Springs, AZ
928-769-2230
www.grandcanyonresort.com
exceptional - $100 up - Cont breakfast - dining - heated salt water
pool & Jacuzzi - pets - Grand Canyon river trips available at
lodge - laundry - nonsmoking rooms - major cards

Grand Canyon Caverns Inn ☆
Mile Marker 115 Route 66
Peach Springs, AZ
928-422-4565 www.grandcanyoncaverns.com
good - $80 - a very special "must stop" - dining - pool - pets -
nonsmoking rooms - coffee makers and internet connections in
rooms - laundry - gas station - mini mart - gift shop - major cards

Frontier Motel
16118 E. Historic Route 66
Truxton, AZ
fair - $65 - dining - pets - a microwave and fridge in one room -
Visa, MC, Disc

Dining:

☞ *All dining establishments in Arizona are nonsmoking.*

Twisters 50's Soda Fountain ☆
417 E. Route 66
Williams, AZ
928-635-0266 www.route66place.com
American - steaks, rib eye, top sirloin, catfish, ribs - exceptional -
a very special "must stop" - liquor - L&D 7 days - atmosphere -
moderate - gift shop - major cards

Cruisers Cafe 66 ☆
233 W. Route 66
Williams, AZ
928-635-2445
American - barbecue, steaks, chicken, pork - exceptional -
a very special "must stop" - moderate - atmosphere - L&D 7
days - liquor - converted 1930s filling station - patio dining -
major cards

Rod's Steak House ☆
301 E. Route 66
Williams, AZ
928-635-2671
American - steaks - exceptional - a very special "must stop" -
L&D Mon. thru Sat. - famous Route 66 icon since 1946 - salad
bar - moderate - liquor - major cards

Rosa's Cantina
411 N. Grand Canyon Blvd.
Williams, AZ
928-635 0708 www.rosascantinarestaurant.com
American/Mexican - good - L&D closed Mon. - moderate -
liquor - smoking on patio only - wi-fi hotspot - mini arcade -
major cards

Doc Holiday's Steakhouse
950 N. Grand Canyon Blvd. (in the Holiday Inn)
Williams, AZ
928-635-4797
American - steaks, seafood - salad bar - exceptional - moderate -
B&D 7 days - liquor - major cards

Pancho McGillicuddy's Mexican Cantina
141 Railroad Ave.
Williams, AZ
928-635-4150 www.panchomcgillicuddys.com
Mexican - barbecue ribs & chicken in the summer - exceptional -
moderate - service - L&D 7 days - liquor - live entertainment -
major cards

Pine Country Restaurant
107 N. Grand Canyon Blvd.
Williams, AZ
928-635-9718 www.pinecountryrestaurant.com
American - homemade - exceptional - value - moderate -
service - B, L&D 7 days - major cards

Ranch House Cafe
111 E. Park Ave.
Ash Fork, AZ
928-637-2710
American - good - inexpensive - B, L&D 7 days - major cards

Westside Lilo's Cafe
22855 W. Route 66
Seligman, AZ
928-422-5456
American/German - exceptional - moderate - service - liquor -
BL&D 7 days - barbecues on the patio during the summer -
entertaiment - smoking on patio only - major cards

Road Kill 66 Cafe & OK Saloon
22830 W. Route 66
Seligman, AZ
928 422-3554
American - exceptional - moderate - L&D 7 days - be prepared
for an "unusual" experience that isn't for everyone - salad bar -
liquor - major cards

Copper Cart Restaurant
103 W. Historic Route 66
Seligman, AZ
928-422-3241
American/Mexican - good - moderate - B, L&D 7 days -
Visa, MC

Snow Cap Drive In ☆
301 E. Chino Ave. (Route 66)
Seligman, AZ
928-422-3291
American - good - a very special "must stop" - inexpensive -
L&D 7 days - no cards

Grand Canyon Caverns Restaurant
Mile Marker 115
(at the entrance to the Caverns, 1 mile off 66)
Peach Springs, AZ
928-422-4565 www.grandcanyoncaverns.com
American - can provide sack breakfasts, lunches & dinners -
good - salad bar - moderate - atmosphere - B, L&D 7 days -
liquor - RV park & campground - major cards

Diamond Creek Restaurant
900 Route 66 (in the Hualapi Lodge)
Peach Springs, AZ
928-769-2800 www.grandcanyonresort.com
American - traditional Hualapi food, tacos & fry bread - good -
B, L&D 7 days - moderate - salad bar - major cards

Frontier Cafe
16118 E. Historic Route 66
Truxton, AZ
American - exceptional - inexpensive - service - B, L&D 7 days -
Visa, MC, Disc

Section 20 - Hackberry, AZ to the outskirts of Needles, CA.

Lodging:

Holiday Inn Express
3031 E. Andy Devine Ave.
(Route 66)
Kingman, AZ
928-718-4393
www.hiexpress.com
good - $99-$120 - full breakfast - pool - microwaves & fridges -
nonsmoking rooms - internet connections, hair dryers and irons
in rooms - fitness center - spa - 24 hr. business center - recently
remodeled - major cards

Best Western Plus - King's Inn & Suites
2930 E. Andy Devine Ave.
(Route 66)
Kingman, AZ
928-753-6101   800-750-6101
www.bestwestern.com/kingsinn
exceptional - $75-$120 - full breakfast - small pets - microwaves
& fridges - pool - laundry - internet connections, irons, hair
dryers and coffee makers in rooms - fitness center - business
center - whirlpool - LCD TV - nonsmoking rooms - major cards

Best Western Plus - A Wayfarer's Inn
2815 E. Andy Devine Ave.
(Route 66)
Kingman, AZ
928-753-6271   800-548-5695
www.bestwestern.com/awayfarersinn
exceptional - $79-$160 - full breakfast - pool - small pets -
microwaves & fridges - sitting area in king rooms - internet
connections, irons and hair dryers in rooms - laundry -
nonsmoking rooms - 37" LCD TVs - major cards

Hill Top Motel
1901 E. Andy Devine Ave.
(Route 66)
Kingman, AZ
928-753-2198
www.hilltopmotelaz.com
good - $40-$75 - pool - dogs only - nonsmoking rooms -
microwaves & fridges - internet connections and hair dryers in
rooms - historic Route 66 motel with small rooms no frills but
clean - major cards

Ramblin Rose Motel
1001 E. Andy Devine Ave.
(Route 66)
Kingman, AZ
928-753-5541
good - $30-$65 - pool - small pets - microwaves & fridges -
nonsmoking rooms - internet and coffee makers in rooms -
weekly rates available - small, no frills rooms but clean -
major cards

Dining:

☞ *All dining establishments in Arizona are nonsmoking.*

Mattina's Ristorante Italiano ☆
318 E. Oak St.
(2 blocks North of Route 66)
Kingman, AZ
928-753-7504
www.MattinasRistorante.com
Scicilian/Italian - seafood, pasta, steaks, homemade desserts - excellent wine cellar - exceptional - value - a special "must stop" - moderate to expensive - atmosphere - service - D Tues. thru Sat. - liquor - in a 112 year old converted house, it has been a retsaurant for 30 years - voted one of the best 25 restaurants in Arizona - major cards

Mr. D'z Route 66 Diner
105 E. Andy Devine Ave. (Route 66)
Kingman, AZ
928-718-0066
mrdzrt66diner.com
American - famous for Mr D'z root beer, hamburgers and the "Harley Hot Dog" - good - atmosphere - service - shakes & malts from the 50s - B, L&D 7 days - diner decor - gift shop - inexpensive - major cards

Roadrunner Cafe
401 W. Beale St.
Kingman, AZ
928-718-2530
American - homemade soups & chili - good - inexpensive - B&L
7am-2pm Mon. thru Fri. - where old 66 and Beale St. converge -
major cards

Oatman Hotel Restaurant & Saloon ☆
181 Main St. (Route 66)
Oatman, AZ
928-768-4408
American - exceptional - value - a very special "must stop" -
buffalo burgers burro ears, homemade "Mother Lode" chili &
stew, sandwiches and salads - LD 7 days (breakfast on
weekends) open 10:30 am til the bar closes - atmosphere -
service - inexpensive - liquor - historic hotel - live music - check
out the unique "expensive" wallpaper - major cards

Olive Oatman Restaurant & Saloon
120 Hwy. 66
Oatman, AZ
928-768-1891
American/Western - Navajo tacos, fry bread, "Burro Breath
Burgers", Wagon Train breakfast specials - good - B&L 7 days -
moderate - major cards

Linda's Cafe
12826 Oatman Hwy. (Route 66)
Topock, AZ
928-768-8011
American - burgers - good - inexpensive - value - B, L&D Wed.
thru Sun. - decorated in Route 66 diner style - Visa, MC

Silver Dollar Chuck Wagon
12907 S. Oatman Hwy.
(Route 66)
Topock, AZ
928-768-9921
American - country style burgers, steaks, ribs, broasted chicken
and omlettes - good - value - BLD 7 days - smoking on outside
patio - liquor - wifi, ATM - Visa & MC

Section 21 - Needles, CA to the outskirts of Amboy, CA.

Lodging:

Fender's River Road Resort
3396 Needles Hwy. / River Road
(Route 66)
Needles, CA
760-326-3423
www.fendersriverroadresort.com
good - $65-$85 - pets - full kitchens - nonsmoking rooms -
fridges - boat launch - nicely situated on the Colorado River -
launching service - laundry - boat & RV parking - no phones in
rooms - major cards

River Valley Inn
1707 Needles Hwy.
(Route 66)
Needles, CA
760-326-3839
good - $30-$60 - pool - pets - microwaves & fridges -
nonsmoking rooms - major cards

Best Western Colorado River Inn
2321 W. Broadway (Route 66)
Needles, CA
760-326-4552
www.bestwestern.com
good - $72 up - sauna & pool - restaurant next door - pets -
microwaves & fridges - free satelite TV in rooms - nonsmoking
rooms - laundry - major cards

Budget Inn
2104 Needles Hwy. (Route 66)
Needles, CA
760-326-2212
www.budget-inn.com
good $30 up - fridges - nonsmoking rooms - internet connections
in rooms - boat parking available - major cards

America's Best Value Inn
1102 E. Broadway (Route 66)
Needles, CA
760-326-4501 www.bestvalueinn.com
exceptional and exceptional value - $40-$80 - Cont. breakfast -
pool - pets - microwaves & fridges - internet connections in
rooms - laundry - free fax & local calls - major cards

Travelers Inn
1195 3rd St. Hill
Needles, CA
760-326-4900
good - $60-$70 - pool - pets - full kitchen - microwaves &
fridges - nonsmoking rooms - WIFI internet connections -
major cards

Days Inn
1215 Hospitality Lane
Needles, CA
760-326-5858
www.daysinn.com
good - $55-$95 - Cont. breakfast - pool - pets - full
kitchen - microwaves & fridges - internet connections in rooms -
major cards

Motel 6
1420 J Street (I-40/US 95 at J Street)
Needles, CA 92363
760-326-3399
www.motel6.com
good - $39 up - Denny's next door - laundry - pool - internet connections in rooms - major cards

Dining:

☞ *All dining establishments in California are nonsmoking.*

Wagon Wheel Restaurant
2420 Needles Hwy.
(Route 66)
Needles, CA
760-326-4361
American - good - B, L&D 7 days - moderate - salad bar - major cards

River City Pizza Co.
819 Broadway (Route 66)
Needles, CA
760-326-9191
American - very good pizzas - good - moderate - L&D 7 days - beer & wine - nights are crowded - delivery to motels - major cards

Juicy's River Cafe
2411 Needles Hwy. (Route 66)
Needles, CA
760-326-0044
American - fish & chips - wide variety - good - moderate - B, L&D 7 days - liquor - major cards

Lucy's Mexican Restaurant
811 Front St.
Needles, CA
760-326-4461
Mexican - good - moderate - L Wed. thru Sun. - a few doors
down from the El Garces Harvey House - major cards

Section 22 - Amboy, CA to the outskirts of Barstow, CA.

Lodging:

Ludlow Motel
6831 Ludlow Rd.
(Route 66)
Ludlow, CA
760-733-4338
good - $50-$63 - next to the Ludlow Cafe - no frills but very
clean, comfortable rooms - check in at the Chevron Station - pets
$10 a night - free direct TV - Visa, MC

Dining:

☞ *All dining establishments in California are nonsmoking.*

Ludlow Cafe
6835 Ludlow Rd.
(Route 66)
Ludlow, CA
760-733-4501
American - French dip, porterhouse steaks, large ham steak
breakfast - good - value - B, L&D 7 days - moderate - historic
marker - nice display of historic pictures of early Ludlow and
Route 66 - Visa, MC

Bagdad Cafe ☆
46548 National Trails Hwy.
(Route 66)
Newberry Springs, CA
760-257-3101
American - buffalo burgers, great steaks - good - value - a very
special "must stop" - atmosphere - service - B, L&D 7 days, call
for hours - a landmark where the movie "Bagdad Cafe" was
filmed - inexpensive - beer & wine - decor features Route 66
memorabilia - Visa, MC

Section 23 - Barstow, CA to the outskirts of Claremont, CA.

Lodging:

Best Western Desert Villa Inn
1984 E. Main St. (Route 66)
Barstow, CA
760-256-1781
good - $81-$119 - Cont. breakfast - dogs only - pool - fridges &
microwaves - internet connections, irons & hairdryers in rooms -
laundry - safes available - nonsmoking rooms - major cards

Holiday Inn Express/Route 66
1861 W. Main St. (Route 66)
Barstow, CA
760-256-1300
exceptional - $109 up - Cont. breakfast - pool - pets - internet
connections, microwaves, fridges, irons, DVD players, coffee
makers & hair dryers in rooms - fitness center - nonsmoking
rooms - major cards

Stardust Inn
901 E. Main St. (Route 66)
Barstow, CA
760-256-7116
good - $40-60 - value - pool - pets - internet connections,
microwaves & fridges in rooms - nonsmoking rooms -
major cards

America's Best Value Inn
1350 W. Main St. (Route 66)
Barstow, CA
760-256-8921 www.AmericasBestValueInn.com
good - $49.99-$59.99 - Cont. breakfast - pets - internet
connections, fridges in rooms - some microwaves - cable TV -
major cards

Route 66 Motel
195 W. Main St. (Route 66)
Barstow, CA
760-256-7866
good - $39.95-$49.95 - $5 a day for pets - internet connections in
rooms - microwaves & fridges in some rooms - nonsmoking
rooms - vintage gas signs, gas pumps & classic cars add to the
ambience - nice neon - major cards

New Corral Motel
16937 7th St. (Route 66)
Victorville, CA
760-245-9378
good - $44.94-$53.50 - pets - nonsmoking rooms - internet
connections, fridges & microwaves in rooms - great neon sign -
Visa, MC

Quality Inn & Suites Green Tree
14173 Green Tree Blvd.
(Corner Route 66)
Victorville, CA
760-245-3461
www.choicehotel.com
good - $84.99-$99.99 - full breakfast - dining - pool - pets -
nonsmoking rooms - internet connections, coffee makers, fridges
& microwaves in rooms - jacuzzi - laundry - gift shop - hair
salon - Avis Rental Car station - major cards

Wigwam Motel ☆
2728 W. Foothill Blvd. (Route 66)
Rialto, CA
909-875-3005
www.wigwammotel.com
exceptional - Cyrus Avery Award winner - $66-$88 - historic,
beautifully and completely restored - this is one of the two
famous Wigwam Motels on Route 66 - since 1949 - pool - internet
connections, hair dryers & irons - fridges - nonsmoking rooms - a
very special "must stop" - gift shop - barbecue grill - major cards

Dining:

☞ *All dining establishments in California are nonsmoking.*

Route 66 Pizza Palace
2040 W. Main St.
(Route 66)
Barstow, CA
760-256-2207
Italian - good - moderate - L&D 7 days - salad bar - beer & wine -
photos on the walls from the Route's heyday - no checks -
major cards

Canton Restaurant
1300 W. Main St.
(Route 66)
Barstow, CA
760-256-9565
American/Chinese - good - moderate - B, L&D 7 days 8 am to 9
pm - beer & wine and limited liquor - major cards

Di Napoli's Fire House
1358 E. Main St. (Route 66)
Barstow, CA
760-256-1094
Italian - good - moderate - L&D 11 am to 9 pm, closed Sun. -
liquor - no checks - much fire station memorabilia - major cards

Juan Pollo
413 E. Main St.
(Route 66)
Barstow, CA
760-255-1166
www.juanpollo.com
good - value - moderate - B, L&D 7 days - the owner of this
restaurant chain is a major Route 66 supporter who also owns
the town of Amboy, CA - debit cards only

Rosita's
540 W. Main St.
Barstow, CA
760-256-1058
good - Mexican/American - moderate - L&D Tues. thru Sun. -
liquor - major cards

Emma Jean's Holland Burger Cafe ☆
17143 D St. (Route 66)
Victorville, CA
760-243-9938
good - American - home of the Brian Burger - old fashioned
home cooking from scratch - atmosphere - service - a true mom
& pop operation, that has been serving Route 66 travelers since
1947 - a very special "must stop" - B&L closed Sun. - moderate -
beer & wine - featured on the TV show, "Diners, Drive Ins &
Dives" - no cards

Johnny Reb's
15051 Seventh St.
Victorville, CA
760-955-3700 www.johnnyrebs.com
barbecue - good - southern roadhouse style with peanuts on the
floor - moderate - B, L&D 7 days - beer & wine - major cards

Summit Inn ☆
6000 Mariposa Rd.
(I-15 - Oak Hills off ramp) (Route 66)
Oak Hills, CA
760-949-8688
www.theroadwanderer.net/RT66cajon.htm
American - good - large portions - a very special "must stop" -
moderate - B, L&D 7 days - since 1952 - a step back in time - beer
& wine - gift shop - Visa, MC & Disc

Mitla Cafe
602 N. Mt. Vernon Ave. (Route 66)
San Bernardino, CA
909-888-0460
Mexican/American - good - moderate - B, L&D, closed Mon. -
serving Route 66 travelers since 1937 - major cards

Amapola
1279 Baseline St. (corner of Mt. Vernon - Route 66)
San Bernardino, CA
909-884-7509
Mexican - good - moderate - B, L&D 7 days - Visa, MC

Cuca's
119 W. Riverside Ave.
Rialto, CA
909-562-0207
Mexican - good - value - moderate - B, L&D 7 days - beer &
wine - a former railroad depot, much is still original -
major cards

Brothers Pizza
142 E. Foothill Blvd. (Route 66)
Rialto, CA
909-874-1987
Italian - good - moderate - L&D 7 days - beer & wine - major cards

Red Hill Coffee Shop
16757 Foothill Blvd. (Route 66)
Fontana, CA
909-829-1591
American - good - value - inexpensive - B&L 7days - no cards

Sycamore Inn ☆
8318 Foothill Blvd. (Route 66)
Rancho Cucamonga, CA
www.thesycamoreinn.com
909-982-1104
American - exceptional - L&D 7 days - a very special "must stop" - expensive - service - liquor - since 1848 - said to be the oldest eatery on the Route - once a stagecoach stop - reservations suggested - major cards

Magic Lamp Inn ☆
8189 Foothill Blvd. (Route 66)
Rancho Cucamonga, CA
909-981-8659
www.themagiclampinn.com
American - good - a very special "must stop" - liquor - L&D,
closed Mon. - expensive - atmosphere - since 1955 - one of the
few remaining examples of the true California roadhouses that
were situated along Route 66 beginning in the 1940s - check out
the flaming lamp - major cards

The Deli
9671 Foothill Blvd. (Route 66)
Rancho Cucamonga, CA
909-989-8122
American - sandwiches - good - moderate - L&D closed Sun. -
beer & wine - numerous historic pictures of the area, check out
the vintage gas station across the street - no cards

Joey's BBQ
1964 Foothill Blvd. (Route 66)
Upland, CA
909-982-2128
www.joeysbbq.com
American - barbecue - good - atmosphere - L&D 7 days -
major cards

Buffalo Inn ☆
1814 W. Foothill Blvd. (Route 66)
Upland, CA
American - buffalo burgers - good - moderate - atmosphere -
pation with a fire pit - a very special "must stop" - since 1929 -
beer & wine - live music - L&D 7 days - major cards

Section 24 - Claremont, CA to Santa Monica, CA.

Lodging:

Double Tree Hotel/Claremont
555 W. Foothill Blvd.
Claremont, CA
1-800-222-TREE
www.doubletreeclaremont.com
exceptional - $129-$249 - dining - pool - nonsmoking rooms -
internet connections, irons, coffee makers, safes & hair dryers in
rooms - spa - fitness facility - USA Today at your door every
weekday - major cards

Best Western Route 66 Glendora Inn
625 E. Route 66
Glendora, CA
1-800-528-1234
www.BestWestern.com
good - $110-$126 - full breakfast - pool - internet connections, microwaves, fridges, coffee makers, hair dryers & irons in rooms - exercise facility - nonsmoking rooms - laundry - major cards

Saga Motor Hotel ☆
1633 E. Colorado Blvd. (Route 66)
Pasadena, CA
800-793-7242
www.thesagamotorhotel.com
good - $89 up - Cont. breakfast - pool - fridges - nicely preserved example of a 1950's California Route 66 motel - free newspaper - free laundry - internet connections in rooms - a very special "must stop" - major cards

Ramada Plaza Hotel
8585 Santa Monica Blvd. (Route 66)
West Hollywood, CA
310-652-6400 www.ramada.com
good - $149 - $399 - small pets - pool - dining - video games -
parking fee - internet access - irons - hair dryers - free
newspaper - major cards

Best Western Gateway Hotel
1920 Santa Monica Blvd. (Route 66)
Santa Monica, CA
310-829 9100
ww.bestwestern.com
good - $169-$229 - dining - video games - exercise room - free
newspaper - fridges - coffee in rooms - internet access - video
games - major cards

The Georgian
1415 Ocean Ave.
Santa Monica, CA
310-395-9945 www.georgianhotel.com
good - $267 up - circa 1933, historic ocean front hotel - art deco -
many rooms with ocean views - small pets - hair dryers - irons -
near the Santa Monica Pier - free newspaper - afternoon tea -
major cards

Ocean View Hotel
447 Ocean Ave.
Santa Monica, CA
310-458-4888 www.oceanviewsantamonica.com
good - $155-$206 - Cont. breakfast - nonsmoking rooms - internet
connections, coffee makers, irons, safes in rooms - major cards

Dining:

☞ *All dining establishments in California are nonsmoking.*

Flappy Jack's Pancake House & Restaurant
640 W. Route 66
Glendora, CA
626-852-9444 www.flappyjacks.com
American - excellent eggs & pancakes - exceptional -
atmosphere - Route 66 decor - B&L Mon. thru Sat. 6 am to 3 pm,
Sun. 7 am to 3 pm - huge portions, consider splitting a breakfast -
major cards

The Hat
611 West Route 66
Glendora, CA
626-857-0017 www.thehat.com
American - famous pastrami - good - L&D - inexpensive - huge
portions - a sandwich place that is not quite as good as Phillipe
in downtown Los Angeles but worth an early stop on your way
into the city - great neon - drive thru - no cards

Cabrera's
1856 E. Huntington Dr.
(Route 66)
Duarte, CA
626-359-3614
www.cabreras.com
Mexican - good - moderate - BL&D 7 days - beer & wine - major cards

Matt Denny's
145 E. Huntington Dr.
(Route 66)
Arcadia, CA
626-446-1077
www.mattdennys.com
American pub - exceptional - fish dishes and an extremely rich Guiness Pot Pie - beer & wine - moderate - L&D 7 days - in the heart of old downtown Arcadia near multiple lodging options and the world famous Santa Anita Race Track - major cards

Lucky Baldwin's
17 S. Raymond
(just south of Colorado 66)
Pasadena, CA
626-795-0652
www.luckybaldwins.com
English pub - Chicken Curry, soups, Ploughman's Platter, known for fish & chips - fair - over 50 beers on tap - moderate - atmosphere - service - B, L&D Mon. thru Fri. 9:30 am to 2 am, Sat. & Sun. 8 am to 2 am - major cards

Europane
950 Colorado Blvd.
(Route 66)
Pasadena, CA
626-577-1828
bakery - exceptional baked goods & sandwiches - inexpensive - Mon. thru Sat. 7 am to 5:30 pm, Sun. 7 am to 2 pm - no cards

Taco Station
Corner of Green St. & Chester
(1 block off Colorado Blvd. - Route 66)
Mexican - home made tortillas - inexpensive - L&D 7 days - eat outdoors - no cards

Señor Fish
618 Mission St,
South Pasadena, CA
626-403-0145
Also 4803 Eagle Rock Blvd.
Eagle Rock, CA
323-257-7167
www.senor-fish.com
Mexican - exceptional fish tacos - if you have never tried a fish
taco, this is the place - inexpensive - 11 am to 9 pm 7 days -
Visa, MC

Auntie Em's Kitchen ☆
4616 Eagle Rock Blvd.
Eagle Rock, CA
323-255-0800
www.auntieemskitchen.com
exceptional - fresh American - specialize in exceptionally fresh
seasonal foods, therefore the menu is continually revolving
moderate - atmosphere - service - B, L&D 7 days - a very special
"must stop" - locally owned - major cards

Fair Oaks Pharmacy ☆
Corner of Mission and Fair Oaks
(Route 66)
South Pasadena, CA
626-799-1414
www.fairoakspharmacy.net
American - exceptional chili dogs and sandwiches - value -
cozy - gift shop - L&D - opened in 1915 - voted best soda
fountain in the West by Sunset Magazine - moderate - a very
special "must stop" - major cards

Mom's Tamales
3328 Pasadena Ave.
(Route 66 transitional alignment)
Lincoln Heights, CA
323-226-9383
www.momstamales.com
Mexican - to die for tamales - if you have never had a tamale,
this is the place - exceptional - inexpensive - Mon. thru Fri. open
at 7 am, Sat. & Sun. open at 8 am - each day, they stay open until
the tamales run out - featured on the TV show, "Diners, Drive
Ins & Dives" - Visa, MC

The Raymond
1250 S. Fair Oaks
Pasadena, CA
626-441-3136
www.theraymond.com
American/European - exceptional - expensive - reservations
recommended - locally grown, in season foods - continually
changing menu - call for hours - closed Mon. - major cards

Philippe The Original ☆
1001 N. Alameda
(2 blks. off Broadway 66, across from the beautiful and historic
Union train station)
Los Angeles, CA
213-628-3781
www.philippes.com
American - it is said they invented the French Dip sandwich -
dates back to 1908 - exceptional - large menu - a very unique
operation that seats 400 - inexpensive - a very special "must
stop" - usually crowded - no cards

Millie's
3524 Sunset Blvd. (Route 66)
Los Angeles, CA
323-664-0404
American - exceptional - B&L 7:30 am to 4 pm - moderate - one of the the most popular restaurants in this area so it is often crowded - no cards

Les Freres Taix
1911 Sunset Blvd. (Route 66)
Los Angeles, CA
213-484-1265
French Gallic - exceptional - value - moderate to expensive - L&D - atmosphere - liquor - bar - major cards

Formosa Cafe ☆
7156 Santa Monica Blvd.
(Route 66)
Hollywood, CA
213-850-9050
www.formosacafe.com
Pacific Rim dishes - good - D - moderate to expensive - a very special "must stop" - liquor - since 1946, movie stars have mingled here, look for their names on the parking places - next door to the old Warner Bros. studio - Visa, MC, Amex

Barney's Beanery ☆
8447 Santa Monica Blvd. (Route 66)
Los Angeles, CA
323-654-2287
Also at:
99 E. Colorado Blvd.
Pasadena, CA
626-405-9777
www.barneysbeanery.com
American - good - B, L&D - very unique atmosphere - moderate - LA with Route 66 thrown in - a very special "must stop" - a weird, funky, fun hodgepodge of stuff - huge menu - liquor - bar - free validated parking - major cards

Ye Olde King's Head
116 Santa Monica Blvd.
Santa Monica, CA
310-451-1402 yeoldekingshead.com
Traditional British fare - good - moderate - BL&D 7 days 10 am
thru 2 am - Sat. tea 2-5 pm - liquor - gift shop - major cards

Warszawa Restaurant
1414 Lincoln Blvd.
Santa Monica, CA
310-393-8831 www.warszawarestaurant.com
Polish - exceptional - moderate/expensive - atmosphere - in a
nice craftsman style house - D Tues.- Sat. 6 pm-11 pm, Sun.
5 pm-10 pm - liquor - located 2 blks. from the actual terminus of
66 - a very pleasant way to end your Route 66 trip - major cards

Tudor House
1403 Second St.
Santa Monica, CA 310-451-4107
310-451-4107 www.thetudorhouse.com
Traditional British favorites - meat pies, tea sandwiches - great
bakery - grocery - gift shop - exceptional - moderate -
atmosphere - service - B&L 7 days, breakfast Wed. thru Sun. 9
am-5 pm, tea room lunch & afternoon tea Mon. thru Sun. 10:30
am-5 pm, bakery & grocery 10 am-6 pm daily - beer & wine -
major cards

Ocean Avenue Seafood
1401 Ocean Ave.
Santa Monica, CA
(southeast corner at the end of Route 66)
310-394-5669
www.oceanave.com
Italian/seafood - exceptional - L&D - moderate to expensive - casual - liquor - bar - valet parking - ocean view - major card

All proceeds from this guide go to support the Route 66 preservation efforts of the
National Historic Route 66 Federation
P. O. Box 1848, Lake Arrowhead, CA 92352-1848
Phone 909-336-6131 Fax 909-336-1039
Website: www.national66.org
Printed in the U.S.A.